Iain Nelson.

Performance Appraisal REVISITED

Third IPM survey

Phil Long

IPM Information and Advisory Services

First published 1986

Reprinted 1987

Printed in Great Britain by Dotesios Printers Limited
Bradford-on-Avon

British Library Cataloguing Publication Data

Long, Phil
Performance appraisal revisited.——2nd ed.
1. Employees, Rating of
I. Title II. Gill, Deidre
658.3'125'0941 HF5549.5.R3

ISBN 0-85292-367-8

CONTENTS

Page

LIST OF TABLES

Page

		Page

ACKNOWLEDGEMENTS

In presenting this report the Institute would like to express its appreciation to all those personnel practitioners who contributed to the research by completing questionnaires, providing examples of performance review documentation and finding the time to discuss their organizations' performance review systems. Without their tolerance and co-operation this study would not have been possible.

SUMMARY

This survey of performance review systems was carried out during the first half of 1985. Its purpose was to update the two previous IPM surveys on performance appraisal (1973, 1977) and aimed to examine what changes might have taken place; to update existing knowledge on the state of the art as currently practised in the UK and to identify emerging trends. A response rate of 42 per cent gave a survey population of 306 small, medium and large sized organizations across a wide cross-section of industries and services in both private and public sectors.

Main findings

1. The majority (82 per cent) of the 306 participating organizations operated performance review schemes. Fifty six (18 per cent) had no formal schemes and of these 30 had never formally appraised employees. Contrary to popular belief, only one third of non-users were small organizations with less than 1,000 employees. Further analysis of non-users revealed that the largest group was in public administration; half the participating organizations in public administration did not formally appraise employees. However there was a greater dispersion of non-users throughout all industrial groups compared with the previous surveys, perhaps reflecting the current manufacturing slump and shifting organizational management priorities. The main reason given for not conducting performance review was that formal review systems were considered unnecessary and of no advantage.

2. During the past decade there has been a substantial overall increase in performance review for non-management employees: an 18 per cent increase at first line supervisory level, 21 per cent at secretarial and clerical level and, most notable of all, a 22 per cent increase at the skilled manual level. There was scant evidence of performance review for the latter in 1977. One

explanation could be the growing interest in flexible work practices and the multi-skilled manual grade, which job evaluation tends to equate with non-manual technical grades. Organizational moves towards harmonization of employment conditions for all non-management grades could be another reason.

3. In most organizations (73 per cent) a performance review policy had been in existence for more than five years. There was significant evidence of recent renewal or revision of performance review schemes, one third of all current schemes being less than three years old. This suggests there could be a resurgence of organizational interest, perhaps in response to a need for greater efficiency and productivity or simply as part of a general need to review and overhaul an existing scheme.

4. The shift of emphasis in performance review towards concern for current rather than future performance, first detected in 1977, has continued. The most important purposes of performance review now are: to improve current performance, to set performance objectives and to assess training and development needs. The latter has been directed towards 'on-the-job' development and the upgradings of current skills to meet present job demands rather than the development of future potential. This emphasis on the improvement of performance and development in the current job probably reflects business uncertainty and the need to maximize output rather than a sophisticated approach to the raison d'etre of performance review.

5. Despite the resurgence of interest in the concept of performance-related pay , there would not appear to be a general trend in this direction. Forty per cent of organizations gave the assessment of salary increases as one of the main purposes of performance review, compared with 39 per cent in 1977 - virtually

no increase. Only 15 per cent carried out the salary review at the same time as the performance review - again no increase. A very small minority indicated the existence of performance-related remuneration schemes which operated solely for top management. Performance-related pay would appear to be less of a growth area than has been indicated by some remuneration consultants.

6. Although there is no evidence of a renewal of interest in management by objectives, the results-oriented approach to performance review continues to be the most widely used, as evidenced by 63 per cent of the review forms analysed. This technique, however, is mostly used for management jobs. Despite a growing interest in job behaviour-based criteria, trait rating is disappointingly still very much in evidence, although used almost exclusively for non-management performance review. Only 11 per cent of review methods used for management and professional employees included trait rating, which tended to supplement other results-oriented methods. By contrast 89 per cent of the non-management review schemes examined used trait rating, mostly in conjunction with other job-related behavioural criteria, the latter at times being no more than personality trait criteria presented as behavioural statements. Although a relatively recent innovation, performance review for non-management employees appears to be a decade behind management performance review in methodology.

7. Most of the forms examined contained a mixture of both narrative and rating scales, with varying emphasis. The 18 per cent which were primarily narrative mostly required an overall performance rating. Rater bias, halo effect and skewedness of ratings remain perennial problems despite some efforts to reduce them. The overall performance evaluation presents a particular problem for the line manager: namely, how to convert specific ratings or narrative statements into a single valid measurement of employee

performance. Forced distribution of ratings were imposed by 10 per cent of organizations in an attempt to control inflated ratings.

8. The trend toward more openness in performance review has grown in the past decade, totally closed systems now being rare. There were inbuilt procedures in the majority of schemes (92 per cent) to ensure that the individual being reviewed had a chance to read the completed report and in 83 per cent of organizations the dissenting opinions of the individual could be recorded on the report. The recourse to a formal appeals procedure in the event of an unresolved disagreement between reviewer and reviewed was available in only half the participating organizations. This does not appear to be an area to which further attention has been given since the 1970s.

9. The trend toward employee participation has also continued and performance review discussions between the reviewer and the reviewed are an integral part of the majority of present-day review systems. The increased use of results-oriented methods and the emphasis on improving current performance have encouraged a joint problem-solving and developmental approach to the review rather than a judgemental one. Performance review discussions in general appear to take longer than in 1977, an indication perhaps of an increasing awareness of their central role in the performance review process.

10. With the current trend toward more open and participative performance reviews, the need to train managers in how best to approach such situations has become more apparent. Almost all organizations provided guidance notes on the management of the review procedures and 78 per cent provided appraisal skills training, a 22 per cent increase since 1977. Over the past decade there would appear to have been a significant increase in the use of of

role-playing techniques, closed-circuit TV and training films, although they are not yet commonplace. The responsibility for the co-ordination and conduct of appraisal skills workshops is primarily that of the training and personnel functions, only 15 per cent of organizations using external consultants.

11. Joint problem solving requires the positive involvement of the reviewed as well as the reviewer. Only 20 per cent of organizations appeared to have ignored the need to encourage employee participation. Just five organizations offered their non-managerial employees performance review training or induction sessions. The main technique for assisting individual review preparation was the use of interview preparation forms, work sheets or some similar approach (83 per cent). There was little evidence of true self-assessment or self-rating being used as the main review tool, although there were some examples of performance review records which incorporated both self and supervisory assessments. This could be the first tentative step towards the use of multi-raters rather than a single rater - mostly the immediate superior.

12. One of the interesting developments to evolve from the increased employee participation in the performance review discussions is the career counselling review, 69 per cent of organizations providing career counselling for managerial and professional employees. However, much of the training effort arising from performance review has been directed towards the acquisition of new skills to meet new demands in the current job, the upgrading of specific job skills to maintain the current job or remedial training to lift performance which barely meets basic job requirements. The focus on marginal or just adequate performance has sharpened, organizations no longer being able to carry underperformers. There were signs that in a few organizations,

line managers are now being encouraged to face up to this issue and to take some action. It is hoped that the emphasis on joint problem solving in performance review should make it less difficult to discuss individual weaknesses.

13. The practice of combining performance and potential reviews has declined notably during the past decade. Forty per cent of the performance review documentation analysed contained no reference to potential, a significant increase since 1977. One reason could be that more organizations are ignoring the question of potential because of declining opportunities for promotion. Alternatively, it could be that organizations have developed completely separate procedures for assessing potential.

14. The assessment of management potential still appears to rely on purely subjective methods, although there has been some increase in the use of assessment centres (18 per cent) and psychological testing - 15 per cent by external consultants and 17 per cent by in-house specialists. This compares with only four per cent for all three methods in 1977. The increased use of assessment centres over the past decade would not appear to be very significant but there is a growing interest. Costs in terms of financial and human resources are a major drawback. Only 11 per cent of organizations had attempted to validate their potential review methods; this, regrettably, did not appear to be an area of concern for the majority.

15. The perceived main weaknesses in performance review remain unequal standards of assessment, some lack of commitment among line managers and some lack of follow-up on action, training and development plans or recommendations. There is a growing awareness of the need to consult and involve line managers much more in the design and implementation of new or revised schemes

if they are to be viable. 'Ready made' systems imported from other organizations rarely function satisfactorily, partly because of organizational cultural differences. Commitment and strong support from top management was also seen as essential to the 'success' of any performance review system. It was seen as equally important that top management should clarify their objectives for performance review as these will influence the type of system required. Unless a performance review system attempts to meet the needs of the individual, line managers and the organization it is likely to fail through lack of support.

16. Despite all its shortcomings, performance review remains firmly established among other basic organizational systems and the past decade has seen no decline in its use. There have been some changes in practice, although more evolutionary than revolutionary. There are distinct signs of a narrowing of the gap between theory and practice in the review process but a wide gap still remains with regard to methods.

1 INTRODUCTION

Performance appraisal is probably one of the oldest yet still most imperfect of managerial activities. It has been the subject of an abundance of research and literature over the past few decades and has been described by Fletcher and Williams (1985)[1] as one of the great growth industries of the 1960s and early 1970s. Yet as Banks and Murphy (1985)[2] observe, despite advances in appraisal technology, effective performance appraisal in organizations continues to be a compelling but unrealized goal. In practice performance appraisal remains, frustratingly, one of the weaker aspects of management, its Achilles heel (Meidan 1981)[3].

Rise and fall of MBO

Although there is still a wide gap between theory and practice this does not imply that there have been no changes in management thinking. Since McGregor's famous critique of performance appraisal (1957)[4] in which he questioned the use of subjective judgements on personality traits and his subsequent adaptation of Drucker's ideas on management by objectives (MBO)[5] as a new approach, there has been a slow but steady shift in emphasis away from trait-oriented schemes toward more results-oriented ones. The MBO approach itself gained considerable popularity by the end of the 1960s but as an appraisal technique it is not without its limitations and interest in its use in the UK waned during the 1970s.

There are certain problems inherent in the MBO philosophy which affect the most well-implemented schemes. Levinson (1972)[6] pointed out the implicit reward-punishment psychology which could be potentially destructive; while Koontz (1972)[7] and others considered that there was a danger of overemphasis on a few major objectives to the neglect of other aspects, such as managerial skills. Other well-documented problems are the focussing of attention on the number of objectives achieved rather than on the level of difficulty and the inability of some managers to select measurements which are neither ambiguous nor beyond the control of the employee (Yager 1981)[8]. The advantage of MBO in relation to performance appraisal is that it is a powerful means of clarifying job requirements and documenting shared expectations, serving as a logical starting point for a later performance review. It is not that the technique has failed but, as pointed out by Graves (1982)[9], MBO per se simply is not performance appraisal. Despite these criticisms and weaknesses in practice, it seems to have been generally accepted that the evaluation of performance against pre-set targets, jointly identified by superior and subordinate, offers a promising approach to appraisal and in sophisticated organizations the trend toward results-oriented schemes has continued over the past decade.

In conjunction with this development there has been a growing interest in a more participative style and the involvement of the individual in the assessment of jointly set targets and objectives. The ideas behind this fairly recent innovation are not new. As long ago as 1957 McGregor[10] was arguing for a performance review system which would give the subordinate more initiative in analysing his or her own performance.

Self-assessment

Some have gone further and advocated self-appraisal. However self-appraisal is not without its own problems, the major criticism being a strong leniency error. In his review, Thornton (1980)[11] also points out that inflated self-evaluation and low correspondence with supervisory appraisals make for difficult performance review discussions, although Meyer (1980)[12] found that in the context of the review discussion, subordinates' self-appraisals were surprisingly modest. Nevertheless the majority of research evidence suggests that individuals hold significantly different views of their own job performance from those held by others. Fletcher and Williams (1985)[13] raise the question whether one set of ratings, eg by supervisors, is necessarily more or less accurate than another set such as those of the appraisee or by peers: a question to which he admits there is no simple answer.

Persistent problems

Other issues such as bias, reliability and validity remain major and persistent problems in most appraisal systems. Bias in performance appraisal is a problem as old as the procedure itself. As early as the third century AD, the Imperial Rater employed by the emperors of the Wein Dynasty to evaluate the performance of the official family members, was criticized for rating according to his likes and dislikes and not according to merit! (Patten 1977)[14]. The issue of validity has long been of interest to academic researchers. There are a variety of theoretical concepts about validity but basically it is concerned with the question of relevance and the appropriateness of inferences made on the basis of some set of measurements. The validity of these inferences is likely to vary with the different uses and purposes of the measurements. The type of validity of more concern to practitioners than researchers is what Dawis (1980)[15] terms 'practical validity', ie does this procedure do the job it is intended to do? A valid appraisal is one which measures the right criteria to determine performance. If an appraisal procedure attempts to cope with a number of different purposes, some in conflict with each other, then practical validity may be difficult to achieve.

There have been strong arguments against the use of a single method to achieve a variety of organizational-centred and individual-centred purposes (Randell et al 1984)[16] since the techniques, procedures and information required for each are not necessarily the same. Other researchers have also questioned the usefulness of performance appraisal as a multi-purpose foundation for human resource management, (DeVries et al 1980)[17] and in a review of the critical issues in performance appraisal Banner and Graber (1985)[18] doubt whether this is an appropriate role and argue that organizational expectations of an appraisal system may be unrealistic.

In addition to the debate about appraisal methods over the past few decades there has been an equally consuming interest in the appraisal process, eg closed versus open systems, the interview/review discussion, its conduct and the problems arising from it, the value of appraisal skills training, etc. Much of the current interest has centred on the developmental aspects of performance appraisal, with emphasis on counselling and motivation rather than evaluation and judgement. One result of this has been the increasing preference among some practitioners to use the term 'performance review' rather than 'appraisal' since the latter is perceived as judgemental in nature and devoid of concern for individual development and well-being. In essence then, both those responsible for developing and revising organizations' appraisal systems and the hapless appraisers have been faced with a bewildering range of criticisms and recommendations upon which to base their decisions. What has been the outcome of those decisions?

The new IPM survey

Since the last IPM major UK survey (Gill 1977)[19] there have been only a few surveys of organizational appraisal systems and practices. These have mostly been American studies, eg Lacho et al (1979)[20], Catalanello and Hooper (1981)[21], Eichel and Bender (1985)[22], the Bureau of National Affairs (1983)[23]. There has only been one UK study of note, carried out by Walker[24] in 1983 among 23 organizations.

The aim of this third IPM survey then is to examine what changes may have taken place since the previous 1977 survey; to update existing knowledge on the state of the art as currently practised in the UK and to attempt to identify emerging trends.

Sample and method

The survey was carried out among a wide cross-section of industries and services in both private and public sectors, using postal self-completion questionnaires. A 42 per cent response yielded a survey population of 306 small, medium and large-sized organizations. Some follow-up interviews were also carried out. Further details of the sample design and a description of the survey population will be found at Appendix 2.

2 PERFORMANCE REVIEW - SCOPE AND OBJECTIVES

Extent of performance appraisal schemes

For the purposes of the survey, performance appraisal was defined as a procedure which involves the regular use of recorded assessment of an individual's performance and (sometimes) potential. The majority of the 306 participating organizations (82 per cent) operated performance appraisal schemes. Eighteen per cent of organizations (56) had no formal schemes, exactly the same as in the 1977 survey. The distribution by size of organizations with and without schemes is shown below.

Table 1 - Size of organizations with/without performance appraisal schemes

Number of employees	Base	With schemes		Without schemes	
		N	%	N	%
500 or less	42	33	79	9	21
501 - 1,000	39	30	77	9	23
1,001 - 5,000	121	98	81	23	19
5,001 - 10,000	37	31	84	6	16
10,001 - 20,000	19	15	79	4	21
Over 20,000	47	42	89	5	11
All organizations	306	250	82	56	18

Non-response 1 Row %

The one striking feature of the analysis shown in Table 1 is that it dispels the belief that small organizations tend to make less use of performance appraisal than larger ones. An analysis of non-users in comparison with the 1977 findings emphasizes this point.

Table 2 - Size of organizations without schemes

Number of employees		1977		1985	
		N	%	N	%
500 or less		16	31	9	16
501 - 1,000		16	31	9	16
1,001 - 5,000		20	38	23	41
5,001 - 10,000		-	-	6	11
10,001 - 20,000		-	-	4	7
Over 20,000		-	-	5	9
	Base	52		56	
				Col %	

Table 2 shows that 27 per cent of those without performance appraisal schemes were medium to large organizations. This is a significant increase from 1977 when all participating organizations with more than 5,000 employees used performance appraisal. Further analysis by standard industrial classification revealed another intriguing feature about non-users: the largest group were to be found in public administration (see Table 3). In fact half of the participating organizations in public administration did not formally appraise employees.

Another point of interest in Table 3 is the greater dispersion of non-users throughout all industrial groups compared with the concentration in the distributive trades, food, drink and tobacco and other manufacturing industries in 1977. A variety of reasons could be hypothesized to explain the changing profiles of non-user organizations, including the current manufacturing slump and the shift in emphasis of organizational management priorities towards survival.

Table 3 - Distribution of organizations without schemes by standard industrial classification

	1977*		1985	
	N	%	N	%
Mining and quarrying	-	-	1	2
Bricks, pottery, glass, cement	-	-	2	4
Chemical and allied industries	5	9	1	2
Metal processing/goods	-	-	2	4
Mechanical/marine engineering	-	-	8	14
Electrical/electronic engineering	-	-	2	4
Construction	-	-	2	4
Timber and furniture	-	-	1	2
Paper, printing and publishing	-	-	2	4
Textiles, leather, footwear, clothing	-	-	3	5
Other manufacturing industries	16	31	5	9
Food, drink and tobacco	9	18	6	11
Distributive trades	15	29	1	2
Gas, electricity, water	-	-	1	2
Transport and communication	-	-	1	2
Insurance, banking, finance	2	4	-	-
Miscellaneous services	5	9	2	4
Public administration, health	-	-	16	29
Base	52		56	
				Col %

* All standard industrial groups were represented in the 1977 survey

However further analysis revealed that 30 of these organizations (54 per cent) had never operated formal performance appraisal schemes for such reasons as shown in Table 4 (see overleaf).

Table 4 - Reasons for never operating performance appraisal schemes

	N	%
Formal system unnecessary, not advantageous	10	33
Perceived links with pay	2	7
Problems in identifying/defining performance criteria	3	10
Union objections	2	7
Lack of commitment from senior management	2	7
General lack of interest	3	10
Organizational structure	3	10
Time factor	4	13
Not known	3	10
Base	30	

Multi-response Non-response 2 Col %

The main reason for not using formal performance appraisal would appear to be that such systems are perceived as of no advantage. This response did not come from mostly small organizations, as might be expected, 50 per cent were medium sized organizations with 1,000 to 5,000 employees.

Twenty four organizations had ceased to appraise performance formally, 50 per cent between one to five years ago. Only one of these organizations gave the reason of closures and major reorganization. The major causes for disenchantment were lack of support from line managers (25 per cent) and dissatisfaction with the results (25 per cent).

Later in the report some of the main problem areas and factors which can lead to the failure of performance appraisal schemes will be examined.

Who is reviewed

The extent to which performance appraisal programmes are applied within organizations can be appreciated by examining the levels of employees included. Table 5 shows the grades of employees whose performance is regularly reviewed.

Table 5 - Grades of employees reviewed

		Percentage of organizations	
		1977	1985
		%	%
Directors (board level)		*	52
Senior management		80	90
Middle management		90	96
Junior management		91	92
First line supervisor		60	78
Clerical/secretarial		45	66
Skilled/semi-skilled		2	24
Knowledge workers[1]		*	55
Others - eg graduate trainees		*	7
	Base	236	250

* Not available in 1977

[1] Knowledge workers = those who provide professional/ scientific and advisory services

Row %

During the past decade it would appear that organizations have been extending their performance review schemes to include different categories of employee at both ends of the organizational structure. Half of the participating organizations include those at directorate level and a similar proportion review the performance of their professional and scientific staff - areas which should challenge any system. Since 1977 there has been a substantial increase (20 per cent) in the use of performance review at non-management level, including first line supervisors. Twenty two per cent more organizations review secretarial and clerical performance but perhaps the most notable is the inclusion of skilled manual workers by 24 per cent of participating organizations. In 1977 only two per cent involved employees at this level. An analysis by size of organization (Table 6) revealed that small organizations with less than 500 employees and large organizations with over 10,000 were most likely to review skilled manual performance.

Table 6 - Performance review of skilled/semi-skilled manual employees by size of organization

Number of employees	Base	Percentage of organizations
		%
500 or less	33	39
501 - 1,000	30	23
1,001 - 5,000	98	19
5,001 - 10,000	31	16
10,001 - 20,000	15	27
Over 20,000	42	29
Base	250	24
Non-response	1	Row %

One explanation for this phenomenal increase in performance review among skilled manual workers could be the growing interest among small organizations in flexible work practices and the multi-skilled manual grade. Job evaluation tends to equate this grade with non-manual technical grades. Changing social attitudes and organizational moves toward harmonization of conditions for all non-management employees could be another reason. Large organizations with sophisticated personnel policies tend to have universal personnel procedures applicable throughout the organization . Whatever the explanation the finding is interesting and appears to be a growing trend. Eighty per cent of the organizations reviewing skilled manual performance had done so for more than five years. It is also interesting to note that in answer to another question, 26 per cent of organizations said they were intending to extend their review schemes to cover more job levels and other parts of the organization.

Compared with US organizations, however, those in the UK are still lagging behind in the extent of their schemes. The 1983 study of 244 US organizations by the Bureau of National Affairs[25] revealed that 91 per cent included first line supervisors, 88 per cent professional/scientific and office/clerical employees and 63 per cent included production workers (skilled manual) in their appraisal schemes. As previously shown in Table 5, the UK coverage was 78 per cent first line supervisors, 55 per cent knowledge workers (professional/scientific), 66 per cent secretarial/clerical employees and 24 per cent skilled manual workers.

Most performance review schemes (73 per cent) for both management and non-management, including directors and knowledge workers, had been in existence for over five years. An analysis of the length of time that present schemes had been operating showed significant evidence of recent renewal or revision (Table 7).

It will be noted that over a third of all current schemes were less than three years old. This finding suggests there could be a resurgence of organizational interest in the performance appraisal activity, perhaps in response to a need for greater efficiency and productivity or simply as part of a general need to review and overhaul an existing scheme. In a minority of organizations the performance review of graduate trainees appeared to have been the focus of recent attention, nearly half the procedures being less than three years old. A third of the organizations reviewing graduate performance did so twice a year. All other grades of employee tended to be reviewed annually (89 per cent).

Table 7 - Length of time current review schemes operated

Grade of employee	Base	Less than 3 years	Less than 5 years	5 years or more
		%	%	%
Directors	127	35	22	43
Senior management	223	40	19	41
Middle management	241	40	20	40
Junior management	230	37	20	43
First line supervisors	195	35	17	47
Clerical/secretarial	162	33	18	49
Skilled/semi-skilled	61	33	18	49
Knowledge workers	134	34	21	45
Others - graduate trainees	15	47	13	40
	Non-response	10		Row %

Aims and objectives of performance review

The raison d'etre for performance appraisal or review is subject to different interpretations. For the individual to perceive positive benefit from the system it needs to be directed toward the consideration of individual needs. From an organizational perspective performance review needs to be part of the overall strategy, well integrated with other systems, in order to justify the resources expended on it. Consequently organizational expectations of performance review systems tend to be demanding and corporate objectives varied, although not always well defined. As one personnel practitioner observed

> "senior management don't always think out what it is they are trying to achieve with performance review."

An analysis of the main purposes for which performance review is used among participating organizations is shown in Table 8. In 1977 Gill[26] noted a significant decline in the use of performance review for the assessment of potential and it would appear from the analysis that this trend has continued. Although the majority of organizations still consider assessment of potential to be one of the purposes of performance review, there has been a 16 per cent decline in its use in this way. Coupled with less emphasis on the link with career planning, the finding could be interpreted as an indication that some

Table 8 - Main purposes of performance review schemes

	1977	1985
	%	%
To assess training and development needs	96	97
To help improve current performance	92	97
To review past performance	91	98
To assess future potential/promotability	87	71
To assist career planning decisions	81	75
To set performance objectives	57	81
To assess increases or new levels in salary	39	40
Others - eg updating personnel records	*	4
Base	230	250

Multi-response   * Not available in 1977   Col %

heed has been taken of those who caution against the incompatibility of performance and potential reviews (eg Randell et al)[27]. However it is more likely that in the present climate of business uncertainty some organizations are more concerned with the current performance of their employees rather than their future potential in jobs which may never exist. The shift in emphasis toward the need for improvement in current performance was noted in 1977 and the trend has continued, 97 per cent of organizations indicating this purpose of performance review. Further evidence is shown in the substantial increase of 25 per cent in the practice of setting performance objectives, although the growing trend toward results-oriented schemes is obviously reflected in this finding. The most common purpose of review schemes, reviewing past performance (98 per cent), is of course inextricably linked with performance objectives and the identification of areas for improvement. An analysis of the three objectives considered the most important by participating organizations confirmed the increasing preoccupation with the present rather than the future (Table 9).

Table 9 - Most important purposes of performance review schemes - mean scores and standard deviations

	Mean Score*	Standard Deviation	Rank
To help improve current performance	1.5	0.69	1
To set performance objectives	1.9	0.75	2
To review past performance	1.9	0.86	3
To assess training and development needs	2.4	0.67	4

* Range of importance 1 - 3

If it is accepted that setting performance objectives incorporates reviewing the extent to which they are achieved, ie past performance, the above analysis of the most important purposes of performance review can be interpreted as

1 to help improve current performance
2 to set and review performance objectives
3 to assess training and development needs

By comparison the three most important objectives for performance review in 1977 were:

1 to assess training and development needs
2 to help improve current performance
3 to assess future potential/promotability

The shift in emphasis away from the assessment of potential in relation to performance review may account for the slight decline in the importance of identifying training and development needs. The finding should not be interpreted as a sign that organizations are no longer concerned with individual training needs, since this would not necessarily be a true reflection of the current situation. But it would seem that more emphasis is being placed on present rather than future needs, with on-the-job development and upgrading of current skills to meet present day demands rather than the development of future potential. Discussions with personnel practitioners confirmed that the identification of training needs is still initiated in the performance review discussion and 97 per cent of organizations indicated that this was one of the main purposes of performance review.

Links with pay

Despite the resurgence of interest in the concept of performance-related pay there would not appear to be a general trend in this direction. The assessment of salary increases was not seen as one of the main purposes of performance review by the majority of organizations in this survey. Forty per cent indicated this usage compared with 39 per cent in 1977, virtually no increase. Furthermore only 15 per cent carried out the salary review at the same time as the performance review, again a striking similarity with the findings in 1977 (14 per cent). As trends go, this would appear to suggest less of a growth area than has been indicated by some remuneration consultants.

In US organizations performance tends to have a direct relationship with pay. Compensation was the main purpose of performance review in three recent US studies, ie Eichel and Bender (1985)[28] 90 per cent, Bureau of National Affairs (1983)[29] 86 per cent and Lacho et al (1979)[30] 80 per cent. Only one US study, by Catalanello and Hooper (1981)[31], had results similar to this survey, 43 per cent. A 1985 study of merit pay in 125 UK organizations (IDS/IPM)[32] noted that a trend towards providing rewards more closely tied to performance at senior levels of management does exist and that more emphasis is now placed on remuneration arrangements as a key to motivating employees at this level. However the study cautions that the changes to date should not be overstated. A very small minority of respondents to the present survey indicated the existence of performance related remuneration schemes solely for top management and further evidence was available from the interview data. Such schemes, however, tended to be separate from those operating for other grades of employees and the method used was most probably profit performance measurement or direct indexing.

Among the 20 organizations visited, five operated performance review systems which were an integral part of the remuneration package, mostly bonus schemes. In one organization the scheme operated for managerial and professional employees only, although there were plans to extend it to all grades of employee at a later date. The review system used was results-oriented. The other organizations operated highly structured and tightly quantified rating schemes, for as one manager commented, 'points mean money'. In one scheme, operated in a non-unionized organization, the initial salary recommendation was made by the appraising manager. Apart from the inbuilt subjectivity of most rating schemes, the latter practice may be overtly influenced by non-performance criteria (Fossum and Fitch (1985)[33] and tends to be viewed with suspicion among unions. In the 1976 Civil Service study by Anstey et al [34], the authors observe

"The appraisal scheme should not be linked too closely with merit ratings for pay purposes. If trade unions suspect that the appraisal scheme is an indirect means of assessing the pay that various staff merit, they are likely to oppose the scheme and with good reason. One union representative, for example, though personally well disposed to staff appraisal, thought that a likely suspicion among some of his members was that one objective might be to 'enable a manager to decide which of his staff is to get a bonus this year'."

Another of the organizations visited in the present survey had recently abandoned a performance appraisal system linked to merit pay because it had been voted out by the unions.

Although the approach of not directly linking performance and pay is usually considered to be the most preferable, this should not be taken to imply that salary decisions should ignore performance. Apart from those salary systems which are based on annual service increments, there is a tenuous link between performance assessments and salary review in most salary administration systems. It would also seem logical that performance and salary reviews should not be too widely separate in terms of time since the performance data may no longer be relevant. Although a reasonable interval gives a chance for a below average performer to improve and thus avoid being penalized in salary terms, too long a period of time before the salary award creates a situation aptly described by one personnel practitioner as 'last year's performance being talked about this year and paid for next year!' The optimum interval between performance and salary reviews would seem to be between one to six months (Table 10). There appears to have been little change in the administrative sequence since 1977.

Table 10 - Interval of time between performance and salary reviews

	Percentage of organizations	
	1977	1985
Less than one month	3	4
One month or more but less than three months	22	26
Three months or more but less than six months	36	30
Six months or more but less than nine months	10	11
Nine months or more but less than one year	3	1
Variable/not known	*	18
Unrelated	*	10
Base	203	211

* Not available in 1977 Col %

Problems with multi-purpose performance review systems

In their review of performance appraisal DeVries et al (1980)[35] noted that the purposes for which it is used had expanded considerably over the past 25 years. The following uses were all cited in a number of US organizations: administrative decisions such as salary, promotion, retention/discharge, counselling, training and development, human resource planning and validation of selection techniques. Fletcher and Williams (1985)[36] observe that most performance appraisal systems form the central part of the personnel management activity, linking into almost every other aspect of the personnel function. Banner and Braber (1985)[37] point out that performance appraisal is often the only system which organizations use to communicate managerial and organizational expectations of subordinates and to clarify job criteria. All these researchers doubt whether performance appraisal systems can adequately serve numerous different and sometimes conflicting purposes.

This concern about attempting to cover too many objectives had been voiced much earlier by Maier[38] who, as long ago as 1958, warned against the inclusion of the review of current performance, discussion of career development and the communication of salary increase at one time using a single procedure. Randell et al[39] have consistently criticized the tendency in many organizations to design all-embracing monolithic systems which expect line managers to give rewards, improve performance, increase motivation and identify potential through a single procedure. This, they point out, is more than a highly trained specialist could be expected to do! They advocate that reward reviews, performance reviews and potential reviews should be dealt with as three separate activities, 'not only separate in time but also in paperwork, procedure and responsibility'.

It has already been shown that the majority of the participating organizations in this survey did separate performance reviews from reward/salary reviews. The relationship between performance review and potential review and the extent to which organizations have succeeded in separating them will be considered later. One of the resources needed is time, a scarce commodity which is always in demand by a number of conflicting priorities.

3 PERFORMANCE REVIEW - METHODS AND TECHNIQUES

The techniques used to assess and measure performance can be grouped into three general categories: comparative, absolute and outcome or results-oriented.*

Comparative methods

These techniques evaluate the performance of the employees in a work group relative to each other. There are three main procedures for making relative performance judgements: namely, paired comparisons, ranking and forced distribution.

Paired comparisons: in this approach the rater compares every possible pair of the individuals, rating which of the two is the 'better'. The basis for the decision may be in terms of overall job performance or one specific performance trait. A rank order is obtained from the number of times each individual is selected as the better of a pair.

Ranking: this procedure requires the rater to list a group of individuals in order of merit from best to worst. Usually a single global performance trait is used to estimate the employee's overall effectiveness to the organization.

Forced distribution: this is a combination of rating and ranking procedures. Although individuals receive a rating of absolute performance level, they are also assigned to categories or ranked performance levels according to some predetermined distribution, usually a percentage to each category. The percentages are developed to produce a quasi-normal distribution, for example, 10 per cent

---

* Sources: DeVries et al (1980)[40], Landy and Farr (1983)[41], Eichel and Bender (1985)[42], Gill (1977)[43].

'best' performers, 20 per cent above average, 40 per cent average, 20 per cent below average and 10 per cent 'worst'.

Limitations

The major limitation of ranking procedures is that they only yield ordinal information and fail to distinguish between levels of individual performance. Thus it is difficult to judge whether two individuals in adjacent categories or ranks are quite similar or dissimilar in their levels of performance. This problem is not quite so marked with forced distribution, used in association with individual performance reviews. Nevertheless these procedures have only a limited administrative purpose and are virtually useless for individual feedback and development. They are also highly subjective, the rater being given a great deal of latitude to infer what distinguishes levels of effective performance.

Absolute methods

Absolute or criteria referenced methods attempt to describe or evaluate the performance of an individual by reference to some standard or standards of performance and not to other individuals. Techniques include the essay or narrative-type approach, graphic or trait rating scales, checklists, critical incidents and behavioural anchored rating scales.

Narrative approach: this is a description of the individual's work performance and behaviour in the appraiser's own words. The appraiser is usually required to describe individual strengths, weaknesses and potential as well as make suggestions for improvement. This approach may take the form of a free essay or a controlled written report, ie essay-type answers to certain set headings or guidelines. The latter format is increasingly being combined with rating scales (Walker 1983)[44].

The assumption behind the narrative approach is that a candid statement from an appraiser who is knowledgeable about an individual's performance can be just as valid as more formal qualitative methods. Narrative procedures have the advantage that they can provide specific details to individuals regarding their performance.

Limitations

In the free essay format the appraiser is given full discretion to infer what performance data is included or omitted. Even when some guidelines are given, the results can vary in length and content, making comparisons between individual performers virtually impossible. The performance profile will also depend as much on the appraiser's writing skills as on the individual's performance. It has been suggested that narrative reports often tell as much about the appraiser as the appraisee.

Trait rating scales: such scales are usually highly structured and consist of a list of personality traits, eg judgement, initiative, reliability. The rater is required to indicate on a numerical scale the degree to which an individual being appraised possesses these traits. A variation of this is the graphic rating scale which requires the rater to evaluate the individual on each of several defined qualities along a line containing a variety of objectives or on a continuum from 'very high' to 'very low'. The trait rating approach is multi-dimensional as opposed to the undimensional approach of the comparative method but the performance dimensions are usually very broadly defined.

Alphabetical/numerical rating scales: these are usually incorporated into a checklist of job related qualities or behaviours. The rater is required to rate the individual on each of the listed items using a simple scale ranging from high to low performance, eg 1-5 or A-F.

Forced choice rating: this consists of a series of groups of statements about job-related behaviours, some being relatively favourable, other relatively unfavourable. Weights are assigned to each statement based on how favourable or unfavourable it is for successful performance (favourability index). A discrimination score is calculated to indicate how well each statement differentiates between high and low performers. These weights and indices are not known to the rater, who is required to choose the items most (or least) characteristic of the individual being appraised.

Limitations

Although less time consuming to administer, permitting quantitative results to be determined simply, conventional rating scales have been criticized on a number of points. Because they lack specific job-related definitions, rating scales are extremely susceptible to errors such as halo effect, central tendency and inter-rater errors of leniency or strictness. A high degree of inference is required on the part of the rater to make connections between specific observed behaviours and the appropriate general rating dimensions. Evaluating performance by the use of traits creates difficult feedback situations, concentrating on the individual's personality rather than on job performance. The use of traits in performance appraisal systems is in any case considered questionable; traits being only personal characteristics which serve as causes or limitors of performance level and do not constitute performance per se. Although the forced choice technique claims to overcome the halo effect, bias or central tendency, the system is likely to be resented since the final rating values are unknown to the rater.

Critical incident techniques: this method is one of the early attempts to move away from trait rating approaches and was advocated by Flanagan (1957)[45]. The method requires the rater to document positive and negative behavioural events which have occurred during a given review period. It has the advantage of being based on specific examples of observed behaviour and therefore is more suited for use in performance feedback discussions. It is assumed to be more objective than global or trait ratings.

Limitations

While emphasizing the importance of observation and recording, this approach still requires a good deal of inference on the part of the rater to determine which incidents are critical to job performance. The method is very demanding in terms of developmental effect and the recording of incidents is time consuming and burdensome.

Behavioural-based and behavioural-anchored rating scales: these represent a significant movement away from global and trait ratings and attempt to reduce the ambiguity of scale anchors. The most common approach is to replace simple numerical or adjectival anchors with descriptions of actual job behaviours based on some form of job analysis to determine what behaviours actually constitute job performance. Although these scales are more likely to be job relevant and of more use for developmental purposes, they still pose rater problems in determining which actually observed behaviours match specifically anchored performance levels. A major refinement on behaviour scaling techniques is the behaviourally anchored rating scale (BARS). A typical BARS instrument consists of a series of vertical scales, one for each performance dimension, which are anchored by incidents selected as the result of a rigorous and systematic analysis of job requirements. The behavioural anchors are usually worded in a 'could be expected to' format. The rater is not asked whether or not the ratee had been actually observed behaving in the manner indicated by an anchor but to predict or infer behaviour on the basis of the rater's past observations of the ratee's work performance.

Limitations

There is still a problem of inference although less so than with traditional rating methods. Despite the considerable expenditure in time and effort required to implement them, BARS do not necessarily contribute to increased reliability, reduction in leniency or halo effect. There are some suggestions (Landy and Farr)[46] that a lack of rigour in the selection and scaling of anchors creates the same vulnerability to errors as trait rating scales. They also need to be continuously updated and validated to ensure that the behaviours specified are still relevant to the job.

Results-oriented methods

These methods concentrate on specific accomplishments and outcomes achieved as a result of job performance rather than on job behaviours. Job performance is viewed as a series of expected results which can be compared with actual performance results. Evaluation is based on how goals and objectives have been met in relation to predetermined standards. Central to this approach is employee participation, objectives being jointly agreed between superior and subordinate and standards established in advance as the result of discussion and negotiation. Shared goal setting is thought to gain individual commitment to achieve goals and to commit managerial support and the provision of the resources required. Since standards are known, variances can be corrected as they develop. Because it is based on specific outcomes rather than on behaviour, performance evaluation should be less susceptible to bias - or so the exponents of results-oriented methods claim.

Limitations

Goal setting approaches need a high degree of inferential skills, managerial time and effort to implement effectively. They are based partly on assumptions of what can be achieved within a given time-span and to a given standard. A detailed job analysis is necessary to establish key areas and job priorities; a great deal of effort is required to agree performance standards and to define them in clear, reasonable terms.

Output measures are thought to be reliable and unambiguous but, as Landy and Farr[47] point out, this assumption ignores the problems of data collection. Goal accomplishment is influenced by factors outside an employee's control, such as co-workers, supervisors, supplies, economic conditions, etc. A particular output measure is only partially the property of a given individual and responsibility for failure may be difficult to establish. Management jobs tend to be measured in terms of unit objectives rather than individual ones. The feasibility of goal setting for complex jobs has also been questioned and Gruenfield (1981)[48] observed that efforts to set performance standards for most professional employees have proved unsatisfactory, primarily because it is difficult to establish objective criteria against which to measure performance.

There are a variety of results-oriented approaches to performance evaluation but the forerunner was MBO. For the reasons previously discussed, it declined in popularity during the 1970s. Gill (1977)[49], detected a wane in its use in the UK and there would not appear to have been a resurgence of interest (Table 11). A minority of participating organizations in this survey (12 per cent) had operated MBO at some time but had since abandoned it.

*Table 11 - use of MBO**

	Percentage of organizations	
	1977	1985
Used throughout the organization	19	20
Used in some divisions	26	25
Base	236	250
	Col	%

*MBO is defined as 'a process whereby superior and subordinate managers jointly identify common goals; define each individual's major area of responsibility in terms of the results expected of him/her and use these measures as guides for operating the unit and assessing the contribution of each of its members'.

Methods in current use

Sixty per cent of participating organizations provided documentation from their performance review systems, including examples of review forms for different categories of employee with accompanying guidelines for appraisers and, in some instances, for appraisees. In total 247 performance review forms were received, 41 per cent for managerial and professional employees, 25 per cent non-managerial and the remainder for universal use. These forms were analysed to establish which methods of performance review appear to be currently in favour and to detect any changes since the previous 1977 survey.

Table 12 - Analysis of performance review forms

Methods		1977		1985	
		N	%	N	%
Results-oriented		102	57	155	63
Job behaviour-oriented		*		128	52
Personality trait rating		61	34	72	29
Alphabetical/numerical rating		19	11	68	28
Narrative - free essay		2	1	6	2
- controlled written		10	6	108	44
Forced distribution global rating		*		24	10
Unclassifiable		24	13	-	-
	Base	180		247	
*Not available	Multi-response			Col	%

Even allowing for possible differences of interpretation in the content analysis of the 1977 and 1985 documentation, some interesting points arise from the comparative data shown in Table 12. The results-oriented method of performance review continues to be the most widely used and, despite the obvious interest in the use of job behaviour criteria, trait rating is still very much in evidence. However the latter technique seems to be applied mainly to the performance review of non-managerial employees. Only 11 per cent of review methods used for management and professional employees included trait rating, which tended to supplement other results-oriented methods. By contrast 89 per cent of non-managerial review schemes used trait rating, mostly in conjunction with other job-related behavioural criteria. Even the latter appeared at times to be personality trait criteria presented as qualitative behavioural statements. Although a relatively recent innovation, performance review for secretarial, clerical, technical and skilled manual employees appears to be a decade behind management performance review.

The majority of the 1985 review systems were a combination of several approaches, an indication perhaps of an awareness of the limitations of any one method. Many of the forms analysed used both narrative and ratings with varying emphasis. Those which were primarily narrative (18 per cent) mostly required a global performance rating, although not in all instances. The trend toward the use of multiple review techniques was detected by Teel (1980)[50] and by Walker (1983)[51]. The findings of this survey would seem to confirm that the trend is still current.

A small minority of participating organizations (10 per cent) imposed forced distribution ratings on the overall performance evaluation. This is done mainly to facilitate its use for administrative and reward purposes. The overall performance evaluation remains a vexing problem for most organizations, namely how to convert specific ratings or narrative statements into a single valid measurement of employee performance. Some of the organizations interviewed did not consider the problem to be insurmountable and had resorted to a descriptive summary of overall performance. This approach is more likely to occur when the main purpose of performance review is developmental and is separate from the remuneration system. Even then a performance measurement may be required at a later time for salary administration purposes. Some schemes adopt a statistical approach but these are very suspect, especially if based on arithmetic averages of specific ratings. Others use weightings on specific job ratings to arrive at an overall score but this does not eliminate any halo effect or bias. Guidelines to assessors tend to advise that the overall performance evaluation should be a 'balanced review of all the objectives mentioned and describe overall how the individual has performed. The overall rating should reflect the summary and not an arithmetic measure of other ratings given.' The usefulness of such guidance is debateable but as yet there does not appear to be any ideal solution to the problem.

Finally, as in 1977, the review forms were classified according to whether they were predominantly results-oriented or personality oriented. This analysis is shown in Table 13.

Table 13 - Predominant classification of review forms

	1977	1985
	%	%
Primarily results-oriented	42	48
Primarily personality-oriented	19	14
Both	14	15
Neither	24	23
Base	180	247
		Col %

While accepting that in 1985 the majority of the results-oriented schemes were for management/professional grades and that the primarily personality oriented schemes were <u>without exception</u> for non-management grades, there would appear to have been very little real shift in emphasis in the techniques used for performance review. In view of the growing interest in job behaviour-based criteria, this is a rather disappointing finding, especially since about a quarter of all non-management schemes had been operating for less than three years. Only 11 per cent of the review schemes used exclusively for non-management grades did not use trait rating scales and these tended to be simplified versions of the schemes used for the corresponding management and professional grades. However, as DeVries et al (1980)[52] remarked, like any other tool, performance review approaches vary in quality; their effectiveness is predominantly determined by who uses them and how they are used.

4 THE PERFORMANCE REVIEW PROCESS

Changing social attitudes, the trend toward participative styles of management and employee involvement in work-related decision making, plus an increasing trade union interest in the inter-relationship between performance appraisal and other personnel decisions, have influenced the performance appraisal process in the extent to which individuals expect to be informed of their performance evaluation. By their very nature results-oriented procedures demand some minimal level of input from the appraisee regarding both achieved and expected performance. The combined effects of these influencing factors should, in theory, provide the impetus toward the shared ownership of the performance review process by the reviewer and the reviewed. How far is this achieved in practice?

The reviewers

As might be expected the immediate superior features predominantly among the reviewers. In almost all participating organizations, (98 per cent) the immediate superior was responsible for carrying out the performance review.

Table 14 - Those responsible for carrying out performance reviews

	Percentage of organizations	
	1977	1985*
	%	%
Immediate superior	86	98
Immediate superior's superior	7	20
Management development committee	1	1
Base	236	250
*Multi-response		Col %

The analysis in Table 14 would seem to suggest that the immediate superior's superior is now more likely to be involved with the review process than at the time of the previous survey. However the role is almost certainly that of a second level reviewer, except in two per cent of organizations. Further analysis revealed that the involvement of a second level reviewer was customary in almost all participating organizations and that this function was usually performed by the first reviewer's own boss. In the majority of systems the second level reviewer countersigns the completed review document (Table 15), the signature of the first reviewer being obligatory.

The role of the second level reviewer is to provide some safeguard against personal bias and possible reviewing inexperience by reading the completed performance evaluation, adding further comments if necessary and by acting as a point of reference for both reviewer and reviewed. While acknowledging that the second level reviewer now has an integral position in the performance evaluation process, McGuire (1980)[53] suggests that the role could introduce yet further bias by appearing to be a second audience rather than part of the review process. Consequently the principal reviewer feels pressured to evaluate for two audiences, the individual whose performance is being

Table 15 - Those who see/sign completed review forms

		Percentage of organizations
		%
Immediate superior's superior		96
Personnel manager/director		81
Directors/heads of functions		14
Management development committee		15
Training/development managers		12
	Base	250
Multi-response	Col	%

reviewed and the reviewer's own superior, the end result satisfying neither.

Table 15 confirms the almost universal involvement of the next level management as reviewers and, most probably, co-ordinators of the performance review process within specific work groups. The analysis also reveals the involvement of the personnel function. During interviews with personnel practitioners it was emphasized that the personnel role in performance review systems was that of facilitator and monitor, the actual review process being emphatically seen as a line management activity. There appeared to be some slight movement toward the involvement of management development committees in the review process but they are usually concerned with performance data only as it may affect succession planning. This role will be examined in the discussion on potential review.

It will be noted that so far the analysis of those having sight of completed review forms has not included that all-important group, the reviewed. How much access do they have to recorded performance evaluations?

Communication of the performance evaluation

Most of the organizations surveyed would consider that their performance review schemes were democratic and that the emphasis was on the sharing of performance-related information between manager and job-holder. Only eight per cent of organizations operated closed systems in which the individual was not allowed to see the prepared performance report compared with 26 per cent in 1977. It would appear therefore that the trend toward greater openness in performance review has continued to gain momentum. In the vast majority of review systems (92 per cent) there were inbuilt procedures to ensure that the person being reviewed had a chance to read the completed report. However this does not mean that no parts of the review form are confidential. One third of organizations indicated that some parts of the performance report were not disclosed (Table 16).

Table 16 - Openness of the performance review report

	Percentage of organizations	
	1977	1985
	%	%
All parts of review report disclosed	39	64
Some parts not disclosed	35	28
Report not disclosed	26	8
Base	236	250
		Col %

An analysis of the undisclosed parts is shown in Table 17.

Table 17 - Undisclosed parts of the performance review report

	Percentage of organizations	
	1977	1985
	%	%
Future potential/promotion prospects	49	89
Overall rating	15	10
Other	15	1
Non response	21	-
Base*	83	70
*Base = Those organizations where report is disclosed in part		
		Col %

Even allowing for the 21 per cent non-response in 1977, the analysis shown in Table 17 reveals some increase in the non-disclosure of potential and promotion prospects. This may be because of uncertain manpower requirements and the unwillingness to raise employee expectations or in some instances because potential review was the subject of a separate procedure.

In 83 per cent of review schemes there was provision on the completed report for the signature of the individual being reviewed. The signature is meant to signify that the individual has read the review report, but not necessarily agreed with it. This shows considerable improvement since 1977 when only 46 per cent were expected to sign their own reports. More important perhaps is the extent to which individuals are allowed to comment on the assessment, this being more indicative of a participative approach. In 90 per cent of organizations the individual was encouraged to comment on the review and many of the review forms examined included a section allocated for these comments to be recorded. Asked whether a dissenting opinion could be recorded on the form, 83 per cent of organizations indicated that this was permitted. This degree of participation and sharing of information did not necessarily extend to the further comments which may be added at the counter-signatory stage; in only 52 per cent of organizations did the individual receive any feedback on these.

A test of real democracy in performance review is the right of any individual to challenge the accuracy of any given performance evaluation and, in the event of a major disagreement with the reviewer, to appeal the review. In most organizations any disagreement is initially referred to the second level reviewer. In the event of an unresolved disagreement the individual should have recourse to a formal appeals procedure.

This does not appear to be an area to which any further attention has been given since the 1970s (Table 18), although some organizations indicated that the normal grievance procedure could be used if necessary. Perhaps in the present climate of openness and employee participation in the review process it is thought that all disagreements should either be resolved between the two parties before the review is recorded or, if necessary, by the intervention of the second level reviewer, without having to resort to a formal appeal stage. This is certainly what most of those interviewed expected to happen.

Table 18 - Extent of formal appeal procedures for performance review disagreements

	Percentage of organizations	
	1977	1985
	%	%
Formal appeals procedure available		
in all cases	49	51
In some cases	7	6
No formal appeals procedure	44	43
		Col %

However this may be an optimistic view and it could be that some dissenting opinions are not recorded because, as Margerison (1976)[54] pointed out, an individual may feel that in doing so any future career expectations may be jeopardized.

The communication of the performance evaluation by allowing the individual to see, sign, comment on or even retain a copy of the performance evaluation record (52 per cent) does not of itself indicate a full participative approach. The extent to which participation is achieved depends more on how the review discussion is conducted and the contribution of both reviewer and reviewed.

The performance review discussion

Ideally, the performance review discussion should be seen as merely one formal event in a continuum of informal work-related communications between manager and jobholder. The event provides an opportunity to 'take stock' periodically, evaluating what has been achieved, agreeing what next needs to be achieved and considering how best these commitments are to be achieved. If the informal work-related communications have been working well, the emphasis of the formal discussion can be primarily directed toward joint work planning and problem solving. In essence the performance review process is no more than a micro image of the organizational cycle of business planning and review, in which the underlying philosophy is to improve current performance. This objective has already been identified as the main purpose of performance review.

The majority of organizations (88 per cent) indicated that the review discussion was an integral part of the performance review process, with the responsibility for its conduct resting mostly with the immediate superior (Table 19). In 12 per cent of organizations the second level manager was involved in performance discussions, either taking the leading role or a part in follow up discussions.

Table 19 - Those responsible for conducting review discussions

	1977		1985*	
	N	%	N	%
Immediate superior	170	86	203	93
Immediate superior's superior	24	12	27	12
Personnel manager	-	-	5	2
Management development committee	4	2	2	1
Base	198		219	

*Multi-response Col %

One measure of the importance attached to this part of the review process may be deduced from the amount of time devoted to it. For example, to assign no more than half an hour to a work review discussion with an employee at management level would be merely paying 'lip-service' to the whole process. Table 20 shows the approximate length of time taken over review discussions for managerial and non-managerial employees. The analysis must be viewed with some caution since it was not possible for our respondents to offer more than a conjecture on behalf of their line managers.

Table 20 - Approximate time devoted to performance review discussions

		1977	1985	
		%	N	%
Managerial employees				
Half an hour or less		19	6	3
Between half to one hour		34	59	27
Between one and two hours		26	117	53
Over two hours		7	32	15
Not known		14	5	3
	Base	198	219	
Non-managerial employees				
Half an hour or less		25	30	16
Between half to one hour		24	104	55
Between one to two hours		11	49	26
Not known		40	6	3
	Base	198	189	
			Col	%

As might be expected, the time given to a managerial performance review discussion tends generally to be longer than that given to non-managerial staff. On average, a managerial review discussion lasts between one to two hours (53 per cent) compared with less than an hour for non-managerial reviews (71 per cent). This finding was statistically significant ($p < .005$). It will be noted, however, that 26 per cent of respondents estimated that a non-managerial review discussion should take more than an hour. The realism of this estimate is impossible to judge but certainly in comparison to the 1977 findings more time appears to be allocated for employees at this level.

In general, work review discussions would appear to take longer than in 1977 and this may be some indication of an increasing awareness of the central part they play in the performance review process. The effectiveness of such discussions, however, cannot be measured solely by the amount of time devoted to them. Much will depend upon both the content and mode of the review and the skill of the individual manager conducting it. Maier (1958)[55] long since pointed out that one of the major reasons why performance reviews fail to produce positive improvements in job performance has been the lack of managerial skills in conducting the review discussion itself. Although most managers acquire a good deal of experience in interviewing techniques during the course of their everyday activities, the performance review discussion still tends to be approached with as much circumspection by the reviewer as by the reviewed. Rowe's[56] observation (1964) that appraisers are reluctant to appraise and even more reluctant to interview is possibly still valid to a certain extent two decades on. With the current trend towards more openness in performance review and the feedback discussion now the norm, the training of managers in how best to approach such a situation would seem essential. It is not only the interview skills which are important but also an understanding of the role of performance review and what it seeks to achieve. As Allinson (1977)[57] observed, if an appraisal system is to function effectively, all members of an organization should be educated about its purpose.

Appraisal skills training

There would appear to be an increasing awareness among organizations of the need for appraisal skills training. As many as 78 per cent of participating organizations provided formal training for their managers, a 22 per cent increase on the previous 1977 findings. Interestingly, however, 49 per cent did not consider that the absence of formal skills training had an adverse effect on the value of the performance review. Underlying this finding could be a belief that for some managers, for example senior managers, such interventions are unnecessary. But, as Allinson[58] showed in his evaluation study of performance appraisal interview training, managers in mid-career may have more to gain from this type of social skills training and Ivancevich (1979)[59] determined that some type of refresher training intervention is desirable to sustain appraisal skills. An alternative interpretation of the research finding could be a reflection on the calibre of the formal training available. Table 21 shows the extent to which certain well-known techniques are used. In addition, some limited use was made of case studies and discussion papers. Four organizations used programmed packages for their skills training workshops. Almost all organizations (94 per cent) provided guidance notes on the management of the review procedure.

Table 21 - Techniques used in appraisal interviewing skills training

	Training films		Closed circuit TV		Role Playing	
	1977	1985	1977	1985	1977	1985
	%	%	%	%	%	%
Used all the time	19	43	11	37	22	53
Used sometimes	26	41	17	33	25	31
Not used	55	15	72	29	53	15
Not known	-	1	-	1	-	1
Base	111	170	111	170	111	170
						Col %

Over the past decade there would appear to have been a significant increase in the use of role-playing techniques, CCTV and training films in appraisal skills training. This is a very encouraging finding, even though such techniques are not yet commonplace. Role-playing tends to be a common approach to practical training in interviewing skills. As the name implies, the trainee, after instruction, practises the skills in a reconstruction of a real situation with other trainees or selected 'guinea pigs' acting out the role of the interviewee. One of the criticisms levelled against role-playing is that the technique tends to be too limited and rather removed from reality. To overcome this problem*, some prefer to conduct real-life exercises (eg Stewart and Stewart 1972[60] Pryor 1985[61]). This approach was used by two of the organizations visited. Whichever method is used, the feedback is enhanced by the use of CCTV and video playback, especially if the audio cassette remains the possession of the trainee (Randell et al 1984)[62]. Such equipment however tends to be expensive and it was not surprising to find that almost a third of organizations did not use it in their training workshops. Some respondents commented on the impact of restricted budgets on their appraisal skills training programmes and the need to modify them.

Primarily, the responsibility for the co-ordination and conduct of appraisal skills workshops rests with the training and personnel functions (Table 22) with assistance from external consultants in 15 per cent of those organizations providing training.

Table 22 - Responsibility for appraisal skills training

		1977	1985*
		%	%
Training manager/personnel manager		55	91
External consultants		6	15
Others		-	1
Not known/non-response		39	3
	Base	111	170
*Multi-response			Col %

The employment of external consultants for skills training workshops appears to have marginally increased over the past decade. Some of the organizations visited had used consultants to set up and monitor

*For further information on how to manage this and other problems associated with role-playing, see Randell et al (1984) [63]

the original workshops before devolving total responsibility to the training function; another had retained the services of an external consultant to conduct the workshops since their introduction five years ago. Others had enlisted the advice of external experts to develop programmed training packages for use by their training managers.

From the 20 organizations visited and additional comments to the questionnaire survey there was some evidence to suggest that the emphasis of the practical skills sessions was on joint problem solving and counselling - one organization actually referred to the workshop as 'performance review in counselling mode'. The problem solving approach which focuses on job difficulties rather than on the individual jobholder has long been advocated to elicit a favourable attitude towards performance review (eg Fletcher 1973)[64] and to gain a greater willingness to implement any agreed remedial action. Some organizations also used the training workshops to tackle any persistent problem, eg unrealistic target-setting, inflated overall performance ratings.

Joint problem solving implies the participation of both parties, the reviewer and the reviewed, but who initially raises the job problem to be solved? With increasing attention being paid to the need for the reviewer to be adequately prepared for the review discussion, how well prepared is the individual whose performance is being reviewed? While accepting that the majority of reviewers are in turn reviewed and hence should have a good insight into the system, the needs of those without supervisory responsibilities should not be overlooked. What steps are taken to enable the jobholder to make an equal contribution to the job review dscussion?

Employee preparation for the performance review

Central to most results-oriented review schemes is the belief in the motivational value of participatively developed goals, clearly communicated and supported by an accurate perception by the employee of the criteria against which performance will be evaluated. What is perceived by individuals is often more important in influencing behaviour than reality. Individuals function on the basis of perceptions and therefore accurate perceptions of performance evaluation criteria are essential for the motivational objectives of a performance review system. Yet, as Wilsted and Taylor (1978)[65] show in a three-year study of appraisal systems, the individual's perception of the performance criteria often varies widely from that actually employed. A consistently applied review policy is recommended, supported by a well-designed training programme not only to help employees understand how performance is appraised but also to provide intuitive cues for assessing their own performance in a realistic way. However, as Kaye and Krantz (1982)[66] observed, preparing employees for their role in their performance review is the missing link in the performance review process. One spin-off from training employees to become more proactive and self-managing in the review process is the encouragement of increased self-responsibility for what is done 'on-the-job' and an enhancement of the power of the manager/employee team. Twenty two per cent of respondents to this survey regarded improved communications and relationships between manager and employee as one of the main strengths of their performance review process.

Another advantage of encouraging employee participation for the review discussion is, as one personnel practitioner observed, the redressing of any imbalance which may occur. This imbalance may arise because of the lack of first-hand information needed to arrive at a fair assessment of performance or through sheer pressure of managerial time. A manager usually has several reviews to prepare whereas the individual has only one. In an experimental 'employee-driven' performance review scheme, McHenry (1984) [67] showed that appraisees spent more time preparing for the appraisal than appraisers did. Fifty per cent of appraisees in his study spent more than two hours in preparation compared with only four per cent of appraisers. This suggests that increasing positive involvement of the individual in the performance review could lead to a reduction of management time spent on the process, a bonus not to be lightly dismissed. Table 23 outlines the ways in which participating organizations encouraged their employees to prepare for their performance reviews.

Table 23 - Employee preparation for the performance review discussion

	N	%
Use of interview preparation forms	121	55
Self-assessment procedure	61	28
Explanatory notes/guidelines	6	3
Written assessment available prior to review discusssion	3	1
Training/induction sessions	2	1
Informal	25	11
None	20	9
Base	219	

Multi-response Non-response 4 Col %

It will be immediately noted that only two organizations offered training or induction sessions. Further discussions with organizations revealed that five actually provided such sessions for their employees and another organization was giving serious consideration to this need. Although only six respondents reported that review guidelines were made available, there were 34 examples amongst the review documentation submitted.

Self-assessment

The main techniques for assisting individual preparation were by use of interview preparation forms (55 per cent) or self-assessment procedures (28 per cent). These two terms tend to be used synonymously, so it is important to distinguish between them. Self-assessment is a procedure whereby individuals appraise themselves, recording what they consider their performance has been over a given period of time and presenting this, both in writing and through discussion, to their managers. This may be facilitated by providing a structured form and guidelines, a blank version of the review form in current use or even a blank sheet with guidelines. Regardless of the tool used, true self-appraisal implies self-rating and as such is rare. As previously observed, research findings suggest that self-ratings tend to have higher leniency errors than superior ratings and may result in discord between the individual and manager. Frank self-disclosure also requires highly sophisticated interpersonal and management skills on the part of the recipient if the situation is not to be construed as threatening or self-damning. It is also doubtful whether self-assessment can be successfully implemented when the performance review is closely integrated with remuneration - or perceived to be.

The finding that 28 per cent of organizations used self-assessment procedures should therefore be viewed with caution, for it is probable that the majority should more properly be described as performance review preparation. This was certainly the impression gained from an analysis of the self-assessment forms submitted: most of these were, in reality, performance review preparation forms. The latter contain a certain element of self-appraisal but are primarily intended as guides or aide-memoires to enable a useful and constructive work review discussion. The completion of such forms is usually voluntary although there may be considerable persuasion exerted to secure employee co-operation. One personnel practitioner made a point of stressing the importance of this stage of the review process and that any individuals failing to respond would 'get the performance review they deserved'. Mostly, employee preparation forms remain the property of the reviewees and are not put on record unless at the specific request of the individual concerned. Of the 61 organizations claiming to use self-assessment procedures (as opposed to interview preparation) 25 retained copies of the self-completed record for employees' personal files. Among the review documentation available for analysis were examples of performance review records which incorporated both self-assessment and the supervisory assessment. This approach is currently being proposed as a means of bringing more complete information into the review process and is seen as part of a multiple-step decision making process (Bernadin and Beatty 1984)[68].

What Table 23 shows clearly is an increased awareness of the desirability of interviewee preparation (80 per cent). Whether or not employees avail themselves of the opportunity to participate more fully in the review process will depend very much upon the prevailing situation between management and managed and the extent to which the process is perceived as meeting the needs of the individual as well as the organization. As Fletcher and Williams[69] remark, being asked for views about the job and its problems, or the goals for next year and how progress is to be assessed, are all elements of participation but are worth little unless there is a genuine response from the reviewing manager.

Developmental aspects

The acknowledged leniency effect in self-appraisal could result in certain training needs remaining undetected. However research has shown a relative lack of halo effect. Thornton (1980)[70] suggests that the individual is more able to distinguish between specific performance strengths and weaknesses than his or her supervisor. The lower 'halo' in self-appraisal implies a better diagnosis of individual training needs and that such diagnoses could be used as the basis of development planning targeted at unique individual weaknesses. In theory, the role of the individual in identifying these should increase the willingness to implement the action plans needed to remedy them. One of the changes noted by organizations now operating more open and participative review schemes than previously (29 per cent) was a greater commitment to performance improvement and development plans.

Individual employee commitment to performance improvement needs sustaining if the desired goals are to be attained. Jointly agreed action plans infer joint commitment from both manager and subordinate. If action plans remain unfulfilled and no initiatives taken on proposed development plans, then commitment will give way to cynicism and the whole performance review system will lose credibility. Participating organizations were asked what provision was made within the review process to enable the monitoring of action and development plans.

Table 24 - Monitoring of performance improvement and development plans

	N	%
Regular reviews by immediate superior	45	21
Line management responsibility	18	8
Named responsibility	7	3
Dated targets	23	11
Responsibility for training/personnel function	78	37
Involvement of management development committee	4	2
Other	4	2
No formal monitoring	63	29
Base	219	

Multi-response   Non-response 4   Col %

Ideally, the responsibility for ensuring that performance improvement/development plans are carried out should rest with the line manager, thereby emphasizing that one of the key responsibilities of managerial work is the development of subordinates. However, given the time pressures on managerial activities, some organizations prefer to facilitate this responsibility by having monitoring procedures built into their performance review systems. These procedures did not devolve responsibility from line management: 43 per cent of the measures taken directly involved the manager. Such measures included regular intermediate progress reviews (21 per cent) and there was some evidence from the review documentation to suggest that a written summary of the progress review was encouraged. Sixty four per cent of review forms included a section for the recording of any agreed action plans so that, if all other measures failed, there was at least a chance that they would be reviewed at the end of the review period.

In 37 per cent of organizations the monitoring facility was provided by the training and personnel function. It will be recalled that the assessment of training and development needs was an acknowledged purpose of performance review systems and 85 per cent of all review forms examined included recommendations for further training or the identification of training needs. Discussions with 20 organizations confirmed that training schedules tend to be based on the development needs arising from the performance reviews. The monitoring role of the training and personnel function was mainly concerned with facilitating the means to meet training needs. Such means did not always entail formal training courses, line managers being encouraged to initiate on-the-job training/development wherever practical with back-up from the training experts as required. The involvement of management development committees in monitoring was comparatively rare (four organizations). As many as 29 per cent of organizations had no formal monitoring procedures.

At present much of the emphasis on training and development is directed towards enabling the individual to perform more effectively in the current rather than a future job. In this context there are three groups of training requirements: the acquisition of new skills to match new developments within the current job, the acquisition or upgrading of specific job skills to maintain the current job or remedial training to lift performance which barely meets or does not meet basic job requirements. The problem of the marginal performer is discussed briefly below.

The review of marginal performance*

Marginal performance tends to be defined as that which only barely meets the basic job requirements, adequate or 'just satisfactory'. It

*This subject was not included in the questionnaire survey but was raised during the interviews. The data collected therefore has no statistical significance but may provide some ideas on how the problem is being faced by some organizations

is not usually the subject of a formal disciplinary procedure but could become one.* Because of its rather vague definitions it is an issue which can be easily avoided in performance reviews. Any tendency towards overrating also masks the problem, eg an 'average' rating being awarded. It has been shown that raters are often motivated to avoid giving low ratings regardless of the level of performance, especially if the information is likely to have an impact on remuneration (Lazer and Wikstrom 1977)[71] or if a valid evaluation is not seen to have any positive consequences (Feldman 1981)[72]. According to Feldman

> "the best evaluation system imaginable will be useless unless its consequences are meaningful. If, for example, a poor performer must be given a positive evaluation so that he can be transferred, the evaluation system is meaningless. Likewise if a reward system is so structured that the consequences of a very positive or merely adequate evaluation are identical, the time spent developing an accurate, unbiased, highly differentiating system has been largely wasted."

Managers sometimes shirk the responsibility of discussing under-performance with subordinates. As one personnel manager observed, there is much anxiety about the ability to handle the discussion, eg in suggesting there could be an improvement and the need to justify this; in the subordinate's reaction to the assessment, especially if the subordinate is a senior management employee. Stewart and Stewart (1982)[73] point out that it is rare for an organization to have a well thought out policy on poor performers and even rarer to

---

*Since this survey was carried out, ACAS has published its draft consultative code on disciplinary and other procedures which recommends that capability issues, including performance, should be kept separate from conduct issues and be the subject of a separate procedure.

find an organization prepared to train managers to deal with them. When the issue was raised in training courses, it was found that trainers usually 'ducked' it. There was some evidence among the 20 organizations interviewed in this survey to show that the training need is beginning to be recognized and that line managers should be counselled on dealing with marginal or under-performance. In some organizations the subject had been included in their appraisal skills workshops, with encouraging results. There was general agreement that the problem of under-performance should be coped with as it arose and should not be stored up for the annual performance review. One shrewd observation was made that if a manager has allowed an employee to under-perform throughout the year, there is a management problem as well.

From the discussion with organizations it appeared that the focus on marginal or under-performance may have sharpened over the past few years. In situations of low growth, stiff market competition and scaled-down manpower levels, organizations can no longer carry under-performers, the new culture demanding satisfactory performance against job requirements. In addition higher standards of performance are required to meet the challenge of changing markets. This, in turn, calls for greater counselling of individual employees to help them to understand the increased effort required for 'acceptable' standards. With increasing standards and job changes those employees who were considered capable one year may no longer be capable the following year. In instances where a long serving employee has been performing just adequately for years, a crisis may be precipitated as the result of management restructuring or a change of supervisor. All these change situations create added problems for the management of marginal performance.

The reasons for sustained marginal or under-performance are manifold. The individual may lack the abilities required and be incapable of doing the job or be quite capable but lacking the specific job information required. This could be the result of a changing job or a job change. If the individual is inadequately prepared for such organizational instigated changes, the organizational policies may also be guilty of under-performance. Alternatively the level of ability may be too great for the job held, the level of motivation strong but frustrated. This would imply a selection problem. Whatever the reason for poor performance, to try to improve it means

> "trying to understand what it is about the individual in his or her situation that makes poor performance and its resulting low self-esteem" (Stewart and Stewart)[74]

The above observation would seem to bring the onus back to the line manager, at least in the first instance.

When the performance review is mainly used as a developmental tool with the emphasis on joint problem solving and an underlying philosophy of continuous assessment, marginal performance need not become a major problem. Those organizations which had recently revised their review systems to more participative and results-oriented ones were hopeful that this approach would highlight performance problems. The need to pay more attention to improvement in the current job would force managers to face up to the issue. By creating opportunities for employees to get more involved in their own performance review, it should be less difficult to discuss individual weaknesses. Although it is commonly thought that individuals are hostile to criticism, Fletcher (1973)[75] found that in the problem solving approach to the review discussion, the discussion of performance weakness was associated with a higher proportion of favourable reactions to the procedure and produced overall a greater proportion of decisions on post-review action. His study suggests that the topic of performance weaknesses can be discussed without abandoning the problem solving orientation and without creating unfavourable attitudes.

Although the discussions with organizations revealed some growing awareness of the problem and some attempts to face up to it, the following comment from one personnel executive is probably indicative of many review systems:

> "performance appraisal is a routine tool for routine management control, geared to middle and high performers. Exceptions do not really fit into the system."

5 POTENTIAL REVIEW

In their discussion on potential review, Randell et al (1984)[76] observe that the identification of an individual's potential for different kinds and levels of work is probably the most technically difficult aspect of performance assessment and development. How and with what kind of information can future performance be predicted? An organizational requirement exists for predictive judgements to be made for the purposes of forward human resource planning. To this end organizations tend to establish procedures for the identification of potential and promotability; some of these procedures are more 'scientific' than others but most rely to a greater or lesser extent on the judgement of line managers.

Predictions of potential by line managers tend in the main to be based on past performance, the only criteria available to them. Although this may seem a reasonable approach, jobs at higher levels may have different performance demands, which effectively reduce the value of predictions made on past performance. Landy and Farr (1984)[77] advise that such reviews are useless and even harmful unless they are directed towards assessing the adequacy of performance on dimensions which are also present in the anticipated job.

Fournies (1983)[78] considers that placing a value on an individual's future promotability is not only useless but ludicrous unless a target job by title and date of expected promotion is specified, the primary objective being to prepare the individual to be able to fill that specific job at a specified future date. Frequently, though, there is no specific job in question and it is left to the assessing manager to suggest suitable jobs and timing. This approach places an unfair onus on the line manager who, unless very experienced, may have only a limited knowledge of job demands at higher levels than his or her own or of those in different functions. Requiring the line manager to rate potential on a given scale does not add to objectivity, since the basis of such ratings is mostly intuition.

This survey is not primarily concerned with the assessment of potential and promotability, but as such assessment still tends to be linked with performance review, a brief study of organizational practice has been included.

The relationship with performance review

Seventy one per cent of organizations confirmed that the performance review was used to assess potential and promotability, although this was no longer one of the most important purposes of the review process. An examination of the review documentation submitted by 60 per cent of organizations revealed that the assessment of current performance and of potential were combined in some forms and separate in others (Table 25). Scrutiny of the 'potential only' forms indicated that assessment of potential was an entirely separate procedure in those organizations (12 per cent).

Table 25 - Analysis of documentation used for potential review

	1977		1985	
	N	%	N	%
Potential included in performance review form	112	62	117	48
Separate form for potential review	20	11	30	12
No reference to potential	48	27	100	40
Base	180		267	
			Col %	

From the above analysis it would appear that the practice of combining performance and potential reviews has declined notably during the past decade. This finding provides further evidence for the increasing trend for the performance review to concentrate on current performance. There has been a slight increase in the use of a separate form to record the assessment of potential since 1977 and a significant increase ($p < .001$) in performance documentation which contained no reference to potential. The latter could be for two totally different reasons:

(a) more organizations are ignoring the question of potential because of declining opportunities for promotion

(b) more have developed completely separate procedures

Of the total sample 21 organizations confirmed that they operated separate potential review procedures.

Sixty two organizations which used performance review for the assessment of potential and promotability did not disclose this information to the individual jobholder. The reasons for non-disclosure given in the review guidelines were partly because of the genuine uncertainty of future labour requirements but also, in some instances, because of the acknowledged subjectivity of the immediate superior's assessment. This bias is by no means reduced by some of the rating scales the unfortunate assessors are required to use. The following is an example extracted from a performance review form which incorporates the flaws typical of many others.

PROMOTIONAL POTENTIAL

(a) Please tick.

SUITABLE FOR ACCELERATED PROMOTION	PROMOTABLE TO NEXT LEVEL NOW	PROMOTABLE WITHIN ONE YEAR	PROMOTABLE WITHIN 1 TO 2 YEARS	PROMOTABLE IN FORSEEABLE FUTURE	NOT PROMOTABLE IN FORSEEABLE FUTURE

(b) Are there factors which will influence promotion?

IS HE WILLING TO RELOCATE	WITHIN THE REGION	WITHIN THE WHOLE GROUP	ANY EXCEPTIONS	AGE	HEALTH	OTHERS (PLEASE SPECIFY) ANY COMMENTS ON THESE

(c) To what position is he capable of being promoted?

Within 12 months	
Within 2–5 years	
Ultimately	

(d) Any further comments?

Section (a) is an example of a much used form of rating, aptly described by Gill (1977)[79] as the 'this year, next year, sometime, never' approach. As Gill remarked, the idea that any human being can forecast with reasonable accuracy an individual's readiness for promotion beyond one year ahead is almost certainly over-optimistic. Section (c) involves even more 'crystal-ball gazing' and assumes insight and forecasting skills far beyond those to which any self-respecting psychologist would be prepared to admit. Fletcher and Williams (1984)[80] observed that the training of line managers in the assessment of potential is likely to be deficient and there was little evidence in this survey to suggest otherwise. The provision of guidelines on the criteria to use is of limited value since this is open to individual interpretation. Although it is appreciated that the line manager's assessment is only the initial move in a lengthy procedure, such judgements could have a significant influence on an individual's chances for further development and future within the organization. The one redeeming feature of the above example is that it would appear to involve some consideration of the social influences on the individual's career decisions.

The following example, although it does not incorporate a rating scale, is open to the same criticisms but requires even greater divining powers on the effects of training.

1. Potential for Promotion:

This employee * is ready for promotion now.
* will be ready for promotion in ____ years.
* cannot be considered for promotion at present level.

2. Potential for Transfer:

This employee *can/*cannot be considered for posts outside his present work function: and if so, *now/*after ______ years.

If No, will further training fit him for a wider function, and if so, after approximately what period. ____________

If Yes, please indicate possible alternative functions ____________

The example was extracted from a potential review form rather than a performance review summary. Such forms usually incorporate the opinions of both the immediate manager and a second level reviewer, usually the assessor's boss. In some instances, only the opinion of the second level manager is recorded. This can be the source of further error, partly because the knowledge of the particular jobholder may be limited. A very real danger exists if the second level manager happens to be a senior executive because such forecasts of potential tend to become self-fulfilling prophecies. Those labelled as 'high-flyers' are usually well groomed and those who label them tend to be reluctant to admit misjudgement.

No doubt because of the difficulties in making accurate predictions about future performance, this is an area which still leaves much to be desired. But a few organizations are attempting to provide guidance for their line managers. For example, one required illustrations of well-known evaluated jobs when assessing potential in terms of job levels. There were also references to the desirability for consultation with other contacts of the individual jobholder concerned. In the main, forecasting was restricted to no more than the next level job or at the most two levels, ie one level above the immediate superior/assessor. There were also signs that managers are less required to predict beyond the next 12 months. This was especially so in the narrative method. The need for a further career counselling review was often included and this could also be at the request of the individual.

Career counselling

The career counselling review is one of the interesting developments arising from the increasing employee participation in the performance review discussion. Preparation for the discussion often requires some thought on career aspirations and there is a growing tendency to record these on the review summary, together with the assessor's comments. In some of the organizations visited career counselling and development exercises had evolved from this approach. Seventy five per cent of organizations indicated that the performance review was used to assist career planning decisions and 69 per cent provided career counselling for their managerial and professional employees. Not surprisingly, such a service was less likely to be available in small organizations with less than 500 employees, (48 per cent). Table 26 shows those responsible for the provision of careers counselling.

Table 26 - Those responsible for the careers counselling of managerial and professional employees

		N	%
Personnel function		82	48
Management development/training function		31	21
Senior management		24	14
External consultants/careers workshops		29	17
Ad hoc		20	12
Other		9	5
	Base	250	

Multi-response   Non-response 20   Col %

An interesting feature of the above analysis is the use of external consultants and careers workshops, the latter indicating an awareness of the importance of persuading the individual to become more involved in life-planning and self development.

Closely associated with managerial career review procedures is management development and the majority of organizations (79 per cent) had management development policies. Obviously the two systems feed information into each other and one direct link is provided by management development committees. For the purposes of this survey a management development committee was defined as 'a group of two or more managers including the executive responsible for management development, whose purpose is to review the current performance of managers and to take an active part in nominations for management succession'. They appear to be making something of a comeback after a decline in the 1970s (Gill 1977)[81]. Thirty two per cent of participating organizations had such committees, predominantly in medium to large sized organizations.

As seen from Table 27, the members of these committees are mostly drawn from personnel, senior and line management.

Table 27 - Representation on management development committees

	N	%
Personnel manager	71	89
Training/management development manager	8	10
Line managers	63	79
Directors/senior management	28	35
Base	80	

Multi-response Col %

One or two examples of career development review and planning were submitted which showed the involvement of the first and second level reviewer, senior management and personnel management.

Other approaches to potential review

Relatively more 'scientific' approaches than those discussed above involve the use of assessment centres and psychological testing. The assessment centre method involves the multiple assessment of several individuals by a group of trained assessors using a variety of techniques such as real life simulations, tests and group discussions*. Organizations were asked whether or not assessment

*For further discussions on assessment centres see Gill et al (1973)[82] and Stewart and Stewart 1981)[83]. A future IPM study is planned for 1986/87.

centres and psychological testing were used for the identification of management potential.

Table 28 - Methods used for the identification of management potential

	1977	1985
	%	%
Assessment centres	4	18
Psychological testing by external consultants	4	15
Psychological testing by internal specialists	4	17
Base	236	250
		Col %

Table 28 shows evidence of an increasing interest in the use of more objective methods for identifying management potential during the past decade, although they are by no means common. Costs may well have some influence on the still rather limited use of assessment centres, since they are admittedly expensive in both financial and human resources. Another reason could be the need to be convinced of improved results above those achieved by more traditional methods.

The validation of potential review methods was not a procedure with which many organizations appear to concern themselves. Only 11 per cent reported any attempts at comparisons between predicted potential and subsequent job performance (compared with 13 per cent in the 1977 study). This included only seven of the 46 organizations using assessment centres.

Perceived strengths and weaknesses

Some attempt was made in the present study to ascertain the perceived strengths and weaknesses of current methods of potential review. The results were of no statistical significance because of the large percentage of non-response. Caution is therefore required in their interpretation.

Table 29 - Perceived strengths of potential review methods

	N	%
Regular, comprehensive reviews	37	15
Common, concise format	23	9
Linked with organizational/manpower planning and development	69	27
Proven reliability and validity	38	15
Use of objective methods	33	13
Commitment/involvement of top management	52	21
Open, participative system	28	11
Achievement oriented	23	9
Other	21	8
Base	250	

Multi-response Non-response 136 Col %

Perhaps the most curious point to emerge is the belief (among 15 per cent) in proven reliability and validity. This has a rather hollow note to it in view of the previous finding of the almost total absence of validation studies.

The main perceived weaknesses are very similar to those previously discussed, ie subjectivity, uncertainty about relevant criteria, and the demotivating effects of limited opportunities (Table 30).

Table 30 - Perceived weaknesses of potential review methods

	N	%
Subjectivity	72	29
Criteria problems	59	24
Ad hoc approach/no common method	39	16
Negative effects of limited opportunities/inadequate follow-up	52	21
Some lack of commitment	13	5
Self-fulfilling prophecy	11	4
Insufficient training of assessors	8	3
Other	21	9
Base	250	

Multi-response Non-response 112 Col %

6 WHY PERFORMANCE REVIEW SYSTEMS FAIL

There is no such thing as the perfect performance review system. None are infallible, although some are more fallible than others. Some systems, despite flaws, will be managed fairly conscientiously; others, despite elegant design, will receive perfunctory attention and ultimately fail. The relative success or failure of performance review, as with any other organizational system, depends very much upon the attitudinal response it arouses.

Lazer and Wikstrom (1977)[84] comment that there are certain standards or requirements that a performance appraisal system should meet if it is to serve its purpose for the organization using it. A 'good' performance appraisal system must be job-related, reliable, valid for the purposes for which it is being used, standardized in its procedures and practical in its administration. To this could be added the requirement that the system should be suited to the organizational culture; for example, a system based on employee participation and openness would be a non-starter if the organizational culture is authoritarian and non-participative in its approach to other employee-related policies. 'Ready made' performance review systems imported from other organizations rarely function satisfactorily. Their failure is due in part to organizational cultural differences.

Attitudes and perceptions

An attempt was made to ascertain general attitudes toward performance review. The most significant responses to a group of attitudinal statements are shown in Table 31.

In addition respondents were asked for their opinions on the main strengths and weaknesses of their own performance review systems. Content analysis of their diverse comments revealed several areas of agreement, as shown in Tables 32 and 33 (page 64).

Table 31 - Attitudes toward performance review

	Agree	Undecided	Disagree
	%	%	%
Line managers dislike appraisal because it creates a lot of paper work for them	56	10	34
Most appraisal systems suffer from unequal standards applied by different appraisers	77	12	11
Appraisal is of no value unless the appraiser has been formally trained in appraisal interviewing	49	12	39
People often perceive appraisal as a way of getting more money rather than feedback on their performance	41	14	45
Multi-response	Base 250		Row %

Perceived strengths

Approximately half of the respondents considered that one of the main strengths of their performance review systems was that they were *work-related*. These practitioners would appear to agree with the theorists that review systems which concentrate on performance planning and development have an improved chance of positive reactions. One personnel executive commented that the emphasis in performance review in his organization had shifted towards key task areas and performance planning at the beginning of the review period

Table 32 - Perceived main strengths of current performance review systems

	%
Work-related; emphasis on planning, improving and developing performance in current job	54
Openness, participative approach	39
Identification of training and development needs	36
Well established corporate policy, part of organizational culture	31
Practicality, ease of administration	26
Standardized, common guidelines and format	22
Improved communications and relationships between manager and subordinate	22
Multi-response Non-response 33 Base 250	Col %

and that much less importance was attached to the review process itself. This system was not salary-linked. In those organizations with fairly recently introduced results-oriented schemes, personnel practitioners reported that both line management and employees were more positive in their attitudes toward the performance review, even though some minor problems still needed to be solved.

More than a third thought that the 'success' of their review systems lay in their *openness* and emphasis on employee participation while 22 per cent regarded *improved communications and relationships* between manager and subordinate as a 'spin-off' from these more open approaches to performance review. The identification of individual training and development needs was also considered a major strength, (36 per cent).

Twenty six per cent of respondents considered the fact that their review systems were *easy to administer*, with concise simple formats, contributed to their acceptance by line management. There was some agreement (56 per cent) that one cause of negative attitudes towards performance appraisal by line management was an excess of paperwork (Table 31). Too much paperwork can increase the chances of performance review becoming a low priority. If a system is practical, it can be used without undue effort by those who must administer it and will be used by them (Lazer and Wikstrom 1977)[85]. Another strength was perceived in the *standardization of procedures* with common guidelines and format (22 per cent). One multinational organization visited had a universal system which was used in its overseas divisions and subsidiaries as well as its parent organization. The key to its success was seen to be in its flexibility and practicality.

Finally, one third of participants perceived that one of the main strengths of their performance review systems was that they were *part of the organizational culture* and a well established corporate policy. This implies the commitment and support of top management, which increases the perceived relevance of the review system. The majority of the personnel practitioners interviewed stressed the importance of this level of support especially for the successful introduction of a new system. Acceptance demonstrated by appraising and being appraised on the system was seen as an essential role for senior managers. If top management fails to set a 'good example', line managers will get the impression that performance review is not regarded as important. One practitioner commented that performance review is done less well at senior management level, there being some reluctance among directors to discuss performance with their senior managers. At the very least, top management needs to take performance appraisal seriously; to clarify the objectives they hope to achieve and to encourage practices which explicitly fit the prevailing organizational culture.

Perceived weaknesses

Table 33 - Perceived main weaknesses of current performance review systems

	%
Considerable variation in standards of assessment, rater bias	37
Some lack of commitment	20
Some lack of follow up action on recommendations	13
Not standardized throughout organization	11
Considerable variation in quality of feedback interviews	10

Multi-response Non-response 34 Base 250 Col %

The majority of respondents (77 per cent) agreed with the statement that 'most performance appraisal systems suffer from *unequal standards* applied by different appraisers'(Table 31). Table 33 shows that 37 per cent perceived this as one of the main weaknesses in their own review systems. All 'people' measurements by other people contain some degree of subjectivity or bias. However some element of rater bias can be design-induced. Many systems, although utilizing an otherwise acceptable format, force the manager to award a single overall performance rating. Realistically, overall ratings are probably inevitable but they affect the accuracy and balance of the review. As Yager (1981)[86] points out, whenever a single rating is used, it is more a rating of the relationship between the manager and the subordinate than of anything else. Whatever else it might be, performance appraisal is a personal event between two people who have an ongoing relationship.

The role of the line manager is crucial to the success or failure of any performance review system. Some *lack of commitment* by line management was perceived in 20 per cent of participating organizations. This can be due to other work pressures which are seen as taking priority over employee development. One personnel executive, while acknowledging the demands on managerial time, observed that

> "performance review is the core of good management if done well. Managers need to be challenged to face up to the outcomes for their departments if they continually allow work pressures to get in the way of performance and career discussions with their subordinates."

One major contributory factor to line management's lack of commitment towards performance review is the lack of consultation. To gain commitment for what personnel practitioners prefer to regard as strictly a 'managerial activity', it seems only logical that line managers should be consulted in the design of the 'management system' they are expected to put into practice. Those systems which are imposed without consideration of the needs of their users deserve to fail.

It was obvious from discussions with organizations that there is a growing awareness of the desirability of involving line managers in the preparatory stages of the design and implementation of any new or revised performance review system. One organization visited, in which a completely new system had been operating for less than one year, had spent up to two years in discussions, modifications and piloting among line managers before introducing it. Even then this system was only operating at managerial level so that any further flaws could be rectified before it was introduced for the remaining non-managerial grades. A attitude survey among all managerial employees was to be carried out at the end of the first year to assess the reactions of both reviewers and reviewed. During the first trial year consultations had been carried out with non-managerial union representatives to ensure that all the objectives of the scheme were understood and accepted before the final phase was introduced. Similar approaches had been taken in other organizations where recently introduced review systems were in operation.

Lack of follow-up on action plans, training and development plans or recommendations was perceived as a weakness by only 13 per cent of respondents. However, this may cause performance review to lose credibility as far as the individual employee is concerned. Encouragement towards self-development and a more active involvement in the management of the job needs to be reciprocated by a supportive environment. If the agreed 'on-the-job' training or recommended training course is not forthcoming or is delayed too long, the employee will become disillusioned with the whole system, and justifiably so. There was a tendency among some of the personnel practitioners interviewed to assume that line managers would automatically approach them for the information and resources needed to assist them in meeting the training and development needs of their subordinates. Given the wide range of specialities within the personnel function, the source of the required information may not be so obvious to line managers.

Only 10 per cent of respondents thought the *quality of the performance feedback interviews* was a major source of weakness in their review systems. Could this be interpreted as an increasing ability among line managers in the conduct of the discussion? It will be recalled that training in appraisal skills was provided in 78 per cent of participating organizations. The analysis shown in Table 32 could perhaps imply that such training is beginning to pay off.

In search of credibility

From the questionnaire survey and the interviews there was evidence to suggest some concerted efforts by personnel practitioners over the past few years to improve performance review systems and to make them more credible. It will be recalled that one third of participating organizations were currently using systems which had been installed less than three years. The personnel executives interviewed acknowledged that some problems still existed for which solutions were being sought. Mostly however, the modifications tended to be minor; there was a feeling that a new system, once installed and initial problems remedied, should be left alone for a while to allow its users to adapt to it.

There was a general concensus among those interviewed that performance review needs regular monitoring to identify any recurring problems and to enable feedback to top management on its success or otherwise in meeting its objectives. In this way, if and when decisions need to be taken on the revision, modification or even total replacement of the existing scheme, they can be supported by well-informed constructive discussions with senior management. Over half the participating organizations were planning substantial changes: 47 per cent intended to revise their existing review schemes while another four per cent had decided to replace them with totally new schemes. Hopefully the corporate plan will allow adequate time for all the necessary preparatory stages required, for, as Lawler et al (1984) [87] observed,

> "quick fixes that make alterations on forms are no more likely to be successful in performance appraisal than are quick fixes in any other area."

In the final analysis performance appraisal fails through inadequate preparation. This includes insufficient consultation with top management to clarify objectives; insufficient consultation with line management to clarify their needs and insufficient time allowed for induction and appraisal skills training; insufficient consideration of the resources needed for refresher training for line managers, induction training for newly appointed managers and, most importantly, the resources to meet the individual training and development plans arising from the review discussions. Unless a performance appraisal system attempts to meet the needs of the individual, line management and the organization, it is likely to fail through lack of support. If this should happen, there is a personnel problem as well.

CONCLUSIONS

Despite all its shortcomings performance review remains firmly established among other basic organizational systems and the past decade has seen no decline in its use. There have been some changes in practice but these would appear to be evolutionary rather than revolutionary, brought about in response to changing organizational situations and attitudes. There are distinct signs of a narrowing of the gap between theory and practice in the review process although wide gaps still remain with regard to methodology.

The review process has been extended to more non-managerial job levels, including manual jobs. The trend toward more openness noted in the previous 1977 survey has continued, closed systems being the exception rather than the rule. In theory this should lead to greater employee participation and seemingly this has occurred; or rather it has been encouraged by such procedures as employee review preparation. Such developments have increased the awareness of the need for more sophisticated interpersonal skills among appraisers and the provision of appraisal skills training is becoming more common. However it was not possible to gauge the quality and effectiveness of such training.

One of the interesting developments to arise from increased employee participation and a developmental and counselling approach to the performance discussion has been a recognition of the need for separate career counselling reviews and there is some evidence to show that these are happening. The main emphasis of performance review, however, is directed towards the improvement of current performance rather than the future. This trend was first noted in our previous 1977 survey and, if anything, appears to have strengthened over the decade. Although this purpose for performance review has long been advocated by academics, the movement toward it has probably been dictated more by circumstance than theory.

Despite assumptions to the contrary, there is no evidence to show a growth in the use of performance review for the assessment of salary increases and merit awards. Mostly performance and salary reviews are separate in procedure and time, this again being in accordance with the recommendations of the theorists.

Performance review methods do not appear to show any major advances since 1977. Although the trend towards the use of results-oriented schemes has continued to flourish, this method has yet to be implemented effectively at non-managerial job levels. The main obstacle would appear to be the difficulty in agreeing targets and objectives. The criteria for any performance evaluation instrument needs to be based on job analysis and performance standards. The move towards results-oriented schemes has meant that more attention has had to be given to updating job descriptions, highlighting key task areas and agreeing the standards against which these are to be judged. This approach can be applied to all grades of job, not just managerial. There is some small evidence of the beginnings of a movement in this direction, giving a glimmer of hope that at some future date trait ratings may fall into disuse. The increasing interest in job behavioural measurements may also help to eliminate trait ratings.

The problems of rater bias, skewedness and unequal standards continue to bedevil most rating schemes despite some attempts to minimize them. One solution adopted by some organizations has been to abandon their use altogether.

As yet there is little evidence of performance review based on self-assessment or self-rating. However the increasing practice of employee review preparation could, in theory, develop into this approach but this would need a radical change in most organizational cultures. Nor is there much evidence of multi-raters, with the exception of the second and occasional third level reviewer. Peer and team rating are methods which were occasionally discussed rather than practised. A recent US survey of 140 organizations (Bernadin and Klatt 1985)[88] reported similar conclusions, the common practice still being single rater appraisals. One or two organizations visited could foresee changes in organization structure with more emphasis on work teams and autonomous units. In this type of structure it was considered that self-assessment based on feedback from peers, internal and external contacts, productivity indices, etc could possibly be used with some degree of success. Team rating could also be applicable for autonomous work groups. It is already in limited practice in the USA (eg Lanza 1985)[89] but there was no evidence of it in the present survey, although one organization was known to be experimenting with it. As Gilbert (1982)[90] points out, employee performance measurement technology remains at a beginner's level and this is especially true in emerging work environments where the employee must exercise a high degree of discretion in his or her daily activities.

It is difficult to predict the future direction of performance appraisal. DeVries et al (1981)[91] comment that it is rather like going into a tailor's shop to buy a suit for your brother who lives a thousand miles away and is on a diet! Hopefully some of the more enlightened trends detected in this survey will continue to grow, and personnel and line managers alike will continue to strive for improvements in what we described in the introduction to this report as that still most imperfect of managerial activities.

APPENDIX 1

EXAMPLES OF PERFORMANCE REVIEW FORMS

These examples have been included to illustrate some of the different formats in current use. A brief description of each review system and its context is given. The majority of these systems have been either developed or revised recently.

Some of the review forms are complete sets, covering a range of employees; some have been extracted to show an example for a particular grade of employee while others are used for most grades.

Although not included here, guidelines for assessors accompanied all the following examples, the more simplistic the form the more detailed the guidelines. All the related review schemes were supported by some type of appraisal skills training.

Example A

This form is used for a results-oriented scheme in a small manufacturing organization. The scheme applies to all grades of employee except manual and has been in use for about five years. It includes a record of major job objectives with expected and achieved results. Attention is drawn to the job description as an essential component. Another interesting feature is the provision for the recording of a progress review.

The emphasis of the scheme is developmental and guidelines are provided for the jobholder to encourage preparation for the performance review discussion.

SYSTEM CONFIDENTIAL

STAFF PERFORMANCE, APPRAISAL & DEVELOPMENT FORM

Name of Appraisee ....

Job Title ....

Time in appointment ....

Relating to period from ....

to ....

SECTION 1 — MAJOR APPRAISAL

1. Is there an up-to-date Job Description ? ....
   If 'No'', what action wil be taken ?

2. What have been the main achievements since the last appraisal ?

3. What has been done less than satisfactorily during the period? Were there any factors which hindered the achievement of satisfactory results ?

4. If difficulties were experienced, what action points have been agreed for the coming year to enable objectives to be achieved and performance to improve
   (a) by the employee

   (b) by the supervisor/company

SECTION 1 — CONTINUED

5. Does the employee have aspirations beyond the present position ?
   If "Yes", are these realistic in the light of past and present performance ? ....
   ....

   What, if any, action is required to help the employee develop further skills and knowledge relevant to the present post and what career development action is necessary to prepare him/her for possible future appointments ?

6. Overall performance rating

(Please tick)

	OUTSTANDING	Superior work of an exceptionally high standard
	VERY GOOD	Work is highly satisfactory. Regularly displays initiative and strives for improvements
	GOOD	Work is very competently handled. Major tasks satisfactorily completed
	AT STANDARD	Performance satisfactorily meets normal Company requirements
	BELOW STANDARD	Work sometimes fails to meet acceptable standards. Has some notable weaknesses
	TOO EARLY TO ASSESS	Employee is new to this post or the Company. Full review planned at next appraisal

7. Comments of countersigning second level manager

Signature ....

8. Comments of employee

Signature .... Supervisor's signature .... Date ....

SECTION 2

RECORD OF MAJOR JOB OBJECTIVES FOR PERIOD .... TO ....

MAJOR OBJECTIVES	KEY MILESTONES INCLUDING EXPECTED RESULTS	RESULTS ACHIEVED

SECTION 3 — SUPPLEMENTARY APPRAISAL

1. Specific changes in performance since last appraisal (Any change in Overall Performance Rating should be mentioned)

2. Progress made against previous Action Points :

3. Additional Action Points/Training Needs :

Date of appraisal ....

Signature of supervisor ....

4. Comments by Employee :

Signature of employee ....

SECTION 4 — TRAINING ACTION PLAN

Name ....

Job Title ....

For period commencing ....

Training need — Please list specific courses, projects or job training requirements, etc.	**Action*** — who is expected to instigate the necessary action to meet this need and by when?	**Completed training** — indicate that training is complete and state how effective it has been.

Internal courses are developed by and all external courses should be booked through the Personnel Department. Please ensure this form is returned to Personnel on completion of the appraisal so that, where applicable, training needs can be extracted and actioned.

STAFF PERFORMANCE, APPRAISAL & DEVELOPMENT PROGRAMME

PREPARATION FOR REVIEW

TO ....

FROM ....

This confirms our arrangements to hold your next appraisal interview

on .... at .... in ....

The purpose of the appraisal is to review your current work performance as an aid to effective working in the coming period and to assist in your further development.

The aim of the interview is to :-

- .Provide an appraisal of your performance in your job
- .Determine your training needs
- .Consider your ambitions
- .Give you an opportunity to discuss any problems or suggestions you may have that affect your work

In order to obtain maximum benefit from our discussion, it is important you prepare for this meeting because the more you are able to participate the more we will both benefit from it.

The importance of the meeting formally is that we can discuss together your work, agree what can be done to improve your performance in your job and make plans for the development of your career.

I would like you, before the interview, to consider how you would answer the questions listed overleaf. It may help you to make notes to remind you at the interview - they will be for your reference only and you may retain this form afterwards.

1. Have you a clear understanding of the purpose of your job and what is expected of you?

2. How well do you think you have done the job during the period under review?

3. What do you think can be done to help you to improve your performance and prepare you for future advancement :-

   (a) by yourself?

   (b) by your supervisor/manager?

4. What do you think are your particular strengths and weaknesses?

   Are your strengths being utilised to the full in your present job?

   Do your weaknesses affect your performance. If they do, what can be done to rectify them?

5. What are your ambitions?

   Do you want to develop in your present work or are you interested in work elsewhere in the Company?

6. What are your personal targets for the coming year?

Space for notes:

Example B

This form is used in a large multinational organization for a results-oriented scheme, which applies to all grades of employee except manual. The format is standardized throughout the organization but some flexibility in approach is possible. In one division there is much more emphasis on the review discussion and less concern with the paperwork, appraisal skills workshops with 'real-life' exercises having been a regular feature for the past five years.

The format incorporates major job objectives, results being reviewed against pre-set performance standards, and job-behavioural criteria. Factors beyond the control of the jobholder are also taken into consideration. Narrative is accompanied by a rating for each criterion reviewed. A developmental plan with named responsibility is included. For long-tenure employees, personal development workshops are also held.

EMPLOYEE CONFIDENTIAL

CO-2173 (4-80)

APPRAISAL OF PERFORMANCE

DATE ____________________ DATE APPOINTED TO PRESENT POSITION ____________________

NAME ____________________ POSITION ____________________

DIVISION, DEPARTMENT ____________________ SALARY GROUP ________

I. **OBJECTIVES/RESULTS** List major job-related objectives; comment on results in terms of job-related performance standards (e.g., quality and completeness of results, use of resources, cost control, time requirements, degree of supervision required). In addition, comment on any unusual conditions beyond the employee's control which affected performance. Rate results, cite specifically how the results met, exceeded, or failed to meet job objectives and standards. (See rating codes below).

RATING

OBJECTIVE:

RESULTS: ________

OBJECTIVE:

RESULTS: ________

OBJECTIVE:

RESULTS: ________

OBJECTIVE:

RESULTS: ________

II. **OVERALL ACCOMPLISHMENTS:** Evaluate the employee's overall effectiveness in fulfilling the major duties, responsibilities, and objectives of the job. Summarize how the employee met, failed to meet, or exceeded the basic requirements of the job. Consider regular job duties; participation in departmental activities outside the scope of the immediate position, furtherance of unit, division and corporate objectives; efficiency of operations; organizational improvements; company or operating division return on net investment; etc. (use attachment, if needed).

____

Appraisal Instructions: Appraise the employee's performance in accordance with defined codes shown below:

RE — Rarely equalled on performance expectations.

CE — Clearly exceeds job requirements. Contributes significantly to Unit/Company success well beyond job demands.

MR — Meets all job requirements and all expectations, in terms of contribution to the company, which were forecast as a basis for the evaluation of the job. Does not require more help from supervisor and others than is implicit in position description. By definition this is very satisfactory performance in a position in which high standard performance is required.

MM — Marginal performance; does not consistently meet job-related requirements; requires more than minimum help from supervisor and others; problem areas need to be monitored and documented.

FM — Fails to meet job requirements; problem areas need to be monitored and documented.

? — Undetermined: Insufficient knowledge due to short time on job.

NA — Not Applicable.

SED 6.83

III. PERFORMANCE CRITERIA: Evaluate the employee's performance in terms of the job-related knowledge, skills and abilities listed below. Cite specific examples which illustrate the employee's proficiency and effectiveness in applying skills, knowledge and abilities to meet the requirements of the job. Rate effectiveness; describe how behavior met, exceeded, or failed to meet, the requirements of the job.

RATING

PROBLEM SOLVING/DECISION MAKING: Consider conceptual and analytical skills, creativity, judgement in problem solving/decision making; ability to identify opportunities and to solve problems; and soundness of decisions as reflected in results. ________

ADMINISTRATION: Consider how effectively work is planned, organized, communicated, delegated, and controlled. ________

LEADERSHIP/DEVELOPMENT OF OTHERS: Consider skill in supervising and coaching, getting results; developing potential e.g. identifying developmental opportunities, willingness to release subordinates; consider contribution to success of company's affirmative action efforts (U.S.). ________

WORK RELATIONSHIPS: Consider effectiveness in working with other employees to accomplish own objectives, and to contribute to others' objectives. ________

COMMUNICATIONS SKILLS: Consider ability to present ideas and information concisely and effectively, orally and in writing. ________

KNOWLEDGE: Consider depth, breadth, and application of job-related knowledge (e.g., technical, organizational and functional). ________

IV. OVERALL APPRAISAL OF PERFORMANCE: Consider results, overall accomplishments, and performance criteria, assigning more weight to results and accomplishments than to performance criteria, indicate the rating which most accurately characterizes the employee's total performance. ☐

V. DEVELOPMENTAL PLAN

A. Considering the employee's overall effectiveness during the appraisal period, summarize (1) the employee's main strengths in terms of performance criteria (above), and (2) those areas which, if further developed, would strengthen the employee's performance.

B. Based on the above, identify Developmental Objectives for the coming year and specify action plans. Consider specific training programs, developmental experiences, and work assignments to strengthen performance.

DEVELOPMENTAL OBJECTIVE	ACTIONS PLANNED	RESPONSIBILITY	DATE TO BE INITIATED

SUPERVISOR	DATE	SUPERVISOR'S SUPERVISOR	DATE

I discussed the contents of this appraisal with the employee on ________________ 19____

Supervisor's signature ________________________________

Example C

This format is used in a small services organization for a results-oriented scheme, which was recently developed in response to organizational change as a result of major restructuring. The focus of the scheme is on improvement, development and growth within the present job and is not salary linked. No overall performance grading or rating is required.

The review summary record is used for all employees and incorporates a review of achievements, contributory factors to performance, future agreed objectives and comments on past and future training and development. Employee participation is strongly encouraged and an individual preparatory work-sheet is provided. Separate preparatory checklists are provided for assessors and cover management, sales, technical, clerical and administrative employees. The checklists are a mixture of results and behavioural criteria (not included in example).

Private and confidential

Performance appraisal *Interview Record*

Interviewee details

Name

Job title

Grade

Division

Department

Location

Date joined
day month year
19

In current position since
day month year
19

Date of last appraisal
day month year
19

How long worked for interviewer
years months

Interview data

Interviewer's name

Interviewer's position

Date of interview
day month year
19

Period under review
month year
19 to month year 19

Summary of interview

Achievements: record outcome of discussions and joint review of **performance** and **effectiveness** in achieving objectives for period under review.

Contributory factors: indicate factors agreed (by one or both parties) to have contributed to exceptional performance or may have contributed to non-achievement of objectives.

Future objectives

Record objectives for the next 12 months (or more) that were discussed and mutually agreed.

Record dates of any follow up, review or assessment meetings now planned.

Development and training

Record analysis of training/learning during period under review.

Record decisions on future development activities.

Any other comments

Any other remarks, comments or statements by interviewer or interviewee not covered elsewhere.

Signatures

Interviewer	Your signature confirms that you conducted the interview and that this is a record of the discussion and conclusions.	signature	date
Interviewee	Your signature confirms the content of this record as accurate – although you may not necessarily agree with it.	signature	date
Interviewer's manager	Sign here to show that you have discussed this record with the interviewer.	signature	date
Personnel		signature	date

Performance appraisal
Individual work sheet

Appraisal data

Name

This interview will be conducted by

Department/division

In location

An appraisal interview will take place on

day month year 19 time • □am □pm

Period under review

month year 19 to month year 19

Review of achievements

List your main achievements during the period under review. (tasks completed, targets achieved, new routines introduced).

Identify and describe any tasks, achievements that you feel were exceptional/important/successful/significant.

Identify and describe any things not achieved satisfactorily/to your satisfaction. Consider why they were not achieved.

Effectiveness

What particular strengths, personal qualities etc have you shown in achieving these results?

In what way would you like to develop any of these qualities, and/or in what areas do you think you need to remedy deficiencies?

Constraints

Have you encountered any obstacles, constraints or limitations in trying to do your job?

How might the way your job is done/organised/managed, be improved?

Development and training

What in particular, have you learned in this period? (Not only formal courses).

Do you have any abilities, knowledge or skills not being used?

What training/development needs do you forsee for the coming year to help you do your job better?

Career development

You may wish to discuss at the interview your aspirations for the future. Note here things you want to mention.

Example D

This system has been in use, with some modifications, over a period of seven years in an autonomous division of a multinational organization. All monthly paid employees are included in the scheme which is directly linked to an annual bonus award system.

The format is basically a BARS approach, with an MBO element for senior grades. The ratings awarded for each work factor are further weighted according to the weightings assigned in the job profile. Note that the final performance score is awarded by the second level reviewer and not the principal reviewer. The review document is completed after the review discussion, the assessment and bonus award being communicated to the jobholder on a separate occasion.

The document entitled 'self-assessment performance report' does not at first sight appear to be so since the behavioural statements are identical to those of the BARS instrument. However the jobholder is encouraged to use this form to prepare for the review discussion, indicating parts of several statements rather than a single statement for each factor if this approach is thought to reflect performance more accurately. In addition an aide-memoire is prepared.

A potential and development report is completed coincidentally to the performance review.

PERFORMANCE REPORT

Reporting Period – 1st November 19 – 31st October 19

Name:		Location:	Joined:
Division:		Department:	
Degree(s) or Equivalent:	Other Qualifications:		Date of Birth:

SUMMARY OF ACTIVITIES IN REPORTING PERIOD

JOB TITLE	HELD		BRIEF DESCRIPTION OF DUTIES
	From	To	

INSTRUCTIONS FOR COMPLETING PERFORMANCE REPORT

(i) Read each line rating definition carefully. Remember that people do not fit neatly into definitions. The definitions given against each numerical score are not exhaustive but are intended as a guide to realistic, uniform and fair rating.

(ii) Underline the words in the definition of each Work Factor which you consider most appropriate.

(iii) You may award intermediate points between 0 and 20.

(iv) The maximum rating against each factor must not exceed 20.

(v) The total weightings for all sections must add up to 100. Multiply section weighting by Numerical Assessment to obtain total weighted points for each section.

WORK FACTOR PROFILE OF JOB (Delete those inapplicable) (from Page 3 of Job Description)

Section	Factor	Weighting
1	Management by Objectives	40%
2	Job Knowledge	....
3	Quality of Work	....
4	Industry and Application	....
5	Initiative, Innovation and Judgement	....
6	Attitude, Adaptability and Emotional Maturity . . .	....
7	Decision Making	....
8	Leadership, Staff Control, Communication and Delegation	....
	TOTAL	100%

Sept. 1981

SECTION 1

Management by Objectives

This section must be completed for all staff in **Grade 6 and above**. For staff in Grade 5A and below this section need only be completed where objectives have been set.

Except where special circumstances exist the overall Weighting to be applied to Section 1, Management by Objectives, will be 40%.

Weighting Section 1 [ ]

Numerical Assessment Section 1 (from Statement of Objectives sheet) [ ]

Weighting x Assessment

TOTAL: = ...

Description	Score
Objectives significantly surpassed or achieved with considerable effort.	(20 (19 (18
Objectives achieved with good effort or partially achieved with outstanding effort.	(17 (16 (15
Objectives achieved with moderate effort or partially achieved with good effort.	(14 (13 (12 (11 (10
Objectives partially achieved with moderate effort.	(9 (8 (7 (6 (5
Little accomplished – little effort	(4 (3 (2 (1 (0
New employee in Grade 6 or above objectives not set for this year	N/R

1(a) If possible, describe, where necessary, the reasons that objectives were not met in full:

____

____

____

____

SECTION 2

Job Knowledge

(Consider here the theoretical, practical and/or technical knowledge possessed by the incumbent in relation to his present job).

Weighting Section 2 [ ]

Numerical Assessment Section 2 [ ]

Weighting x Assessment

TOTAL: = ...

Description	Score
Has exceptionally wide and up-to-date knowledge of present job and related matters.	(20 (19 (18 (17 (16
Has sound knowledge of job; well informed.	(15 (14 (13 (12 (11
Has sufficient knowledge to cope with job	(10 (9 (8 (7 (6
Has limited knowledge and not too well informed	(5 (4 (3 (2 (1
Despite experience in the job has less knowledge than can be expected. Displays serious weaknesses and/or limitations in essential knowledge	(0
Recently appointed and has incomplete knowledge of job	N/R

2(a) Any other comments concerning Job Knowledge?

____

____

____

2(b) What is being done to overcome the weaknesses if any, in Job Knowledge?

____

____

____

SECTION 3

Quality of Work

(Consider here the thoroughness, accuracy and reliability of the work done).

Weighting Section 3 [ ]

Numerical Assessment Section 3 [ ]

Weighting x Assessment

TOTAL: = ...

Quality of work is of a consistently high standard and reliability.	(20 (19 (18 (17 (16
Quality of work is good and there are few occasions when accuracy, content and/or reliability can be questioned.	(15 (14 (13 (12 (11
Can be relied upon to produce work which in terms of accuracy and reliability is satisfactory.	(10 (9 (8 (7 (6
Quality of work leaves something to be desired in accuracy, presentation and reliability. Can be careless.	(5 (4 (3 (2 (1
Quality of work cannot be relied on, prone to make repeat mistakes.	(0
Recently appointed and too early to judge quality of work.	N/R

3(a) Any other comments concerning Quality of Work?

____

____

____

3(b) What is being done, where necessary, to improve the Quality of Work?

____

____

____

T144

SECTION 4

Industry and Application

(Consider here the volume of **effective work**; the level of diligence, enthusiasm and persistent effort applied to the job).

Weighting Section 4 [ ]

Numerical Assessment Section 4 [ ]

Weighting x Assessment

TOTAL: = ...

Wholehearted commitment, application and dedication to the tasks in hand. Extremely energetic and keen. High and effective work rate.	(20 (19 (18 (17 (16
Hard working, keen and energetic, quick on uptake. Works well without prompting. Above average work rate.	(15 (14 (13 (12 (11
Generally works well but does not stand out as an exceptionally hard working and/or energetic person.	(10 (9 (8 (7 (6
Low output, easily baulked by minor set backs and/or opposition. Inclined to be too easy going. Does sufficient to get by.	(5 (4 (3 (2 (1
Lazy and/or lacking energy. Shows insufficient interest in the job. Neglects work.	(0
Recently appointed and too early to judge Industry and Application	N/R

4(a) Any other comments concerning Industry and Application?

____

____

____

4(b) What is being done, where necessary, to improve Industry and Application?

____

____

____

SECTION 5

Initiative, Innovation and Judgement

(Consider here the ability to analyse problems and evaluate data objectively and form appropriate course of action. Consider also the ability to produce constructive ideas appropriate to his area of operation).

Weighting Section 5 [ ]

Numerical Assessment Section 5 [ ]

Weighting x Assessment

TOTAL: = ...

Description	Score
Demonstrates sound judgement, based on clear common sense thinking and a well developed critical faculty. Not afraid to use iniatiative which is skilfully applied. Resourceful confident and full of ideas.	(20 (19 (18 (17 (16
Good and well balanced judgement demonstrated in difficult situations. Uses initiative sensibly and generally has good ideas.	(15 (14 (13 (12 (11
Judgement is sometimes uncertain. Sometimes hesitates to take initiative. Some ideas but really not an innovator.	(10 (9 (8 (7 (6
Generally avoids the unusual or new situation unless pushed. Normally not prepared to take the initiative. Judgement can be called into question. Often takes the easy way out.	(5 (4 (3 (2 (1
Woolly thinker lacking initiative, and balanced judgement with little or no self confidence, and no ideas.	(0
Recently appointed and too early to judge Initiative, Innovation and Judgement	N/R

5(a) Any other comments concerning Initiative, Innovation and Judgement?

____

____

____

5(b) What is being done, where necessary, to improve Initiative, Innovation and Judgement?

____

____

____

SECTION 6

Attitude, Adaptability, and Emotional Maturity

(Consider here the ability to meet and accept change, the need to work together towards common goals, the behaviour, attitude and manner towards subordinates, colleagues and seniors. Consider also the ability to deal with facts and situations in an objective and unemotional manner).

Weighting Section 6 [ ]

Numerical Assessment Section 6 [ ]

Weighting x Assessment

TOTAL: = ...

Description	Score
Enthusiastic, sincere, loyal, co-operative and completely reliable in every way. Open minded to new ideas and concepts with the ability to deal with facts and situations calmly and in an emotionally mature manner. Neverthe-less not afraid to speak his mind and defend his view force-fully when circumstances demand such an approach.	(20 (19 (18 (17 (16
Conscientious employee who adapts well to new situations. Helpful and cheerful attitude. Emotionally balanced. Easy to work with. Can generally be counted on to express and defend his viewpoint	(15 (14 (13 (12 (11
Generally reliable and co-operative. Copes adequately with most work and people situations. Works reasonably well with most people.	(10 (9 (8 (7 (6
Seldom seen to put himself out. Occasionally loses sense of proprotion and creates situation of friction and tension.	(5 (4 (3 (2 (1
Often unco-operative with a blinkered approach to any new ideas and given to getting things out of proportion.	(0
Recently appointed and too early to judge Attitude, Adaptability and Emotional Maturity.	N/R

6(a) Any other comments concerning Attitude, Adaptability and Emotional Maturity?

____

____

____

6(b) What is being done, where necessary, to improve Attitude, Adaptability and Emotional Maturity?

____

____

____

SECTION 7

Decision Making

(Consider here the quality and promptness of decisions made, together with the acceptance of responsibility for those decisions).

Weighting Section 7

[ ]

Numerical Assessment Section 7

[ ]

Weighting x Assessment

TOTAL: = ...

Description	Score
Prepared to make decisions promptly and takes care to try to make them correctly. Does not shirk the difficult decision but knows when to refer decision making process up the line. Accepts responsibility for his decisions.	(20 (19 (18 (17 (16
Reaches sensible and prompt decisions about most matters in his area of responsibility. Likes to sound out seniors before announcing decision.	(15 (14 (13 (12 (11
Occasionally cannot see wood for trees and refers too many items up the line for decision. Reluctant to accept responsibility for decision. Tends to take too long in reaching decision. Plays for safety.	(10 (9 (8 (7 (6
Finds considerable difficulty in making sound decisions on the simplest of subjects.	(5 (4 (3 (2 (1
Not prepared to make decisions, refers all items up the line.	(0
Recently appointed and too early to judge Decision Making	N/R

7(a) Any other comments concerning Decision Making?

____

____

____

7(b) What is being done, where necessary, to overcome the weaknesses, if any, highlighted by this report?

____

____

____

SECTION 8

Leadership, Staff Control, Communication and Delegation

(Consider here the ability and capacity to motivate, plan, delegate and to establish adequate controls, to organise, to communicate and to co-ordinate. Consider also man management ability).

Weighting Section 8

[ ]

Numerical Assessment Section 8

[ ]

Weighting x Assessment

TOTAL: = ...

Description	Score
Most capable leader, morale in department high. Inspires confidence. Effective and persuasive communicator both up and down. Prepared to delegate responsibility with corresponding authority and helps subordinates to improve and develop.	(20 (19 (18 (17 (16
Controls staff effectively, a good example and influence and a good leader. Demonstrates a clear ability to direct others to reach common goals. Delegates and communicates well.	(15 (14 (13 (12 (11
Generally handles staff well but is happier as a team member rather than a leader. Tries hard to communicate and delegate effectively.	(10 (9 (8 (7 (6
Not always in complete control of section or department. Has difficulty in controlling and leading. Finds delegation difficult.	(5 (4 (3 (2 (1
Has little control over staff, too easy going. Does not inspire confidence. Little or no interest shown in developing subordinates. Communication skills leave much to be desired.	(0
Recently appointed and too early to judge Leadership, Staff Control, Communication and Delegation	N/R

8(a) Any other comments concerning Leadership, Staff Control, Communication and Delegation?

____

____

____

8(b) What is being done, where necessary, to improve Leadership, Staff Control, Communication and Delegation?

____

____

____

9. TOTAL ALL POINTS – **Section 1 to 8 inclusive** . . . . / 2000

Date . . . . Signed Reporting Manager . . . .

10. OVERALL REVIEW AND PERFORMANCE RATING BY NEXT LEVEL OF MANAGEMENT

Final Numerical Rating . . . .

Date . . . . Signed Departmental Head . . . .

The report completed to his Section must be passed to the Personnel Manager

11. APPRAISAL AND COMMUNICATION INTERVIEW RECORD:

Date . . . . Department Head . . . .

12. DIRECTORS OVERALL VIEW:

Date . . . . Director . . . .

POTENTIAL AND DEVELOPMENT REPORT

A. PERSONAL DETAILS

Name : .... Job Title : ....

Age : .... Department : ....

Date joined Co. : .... Job Grade : ....

B. ASSESSMENT OF POTENTIAL (Please mark appropriate box)

☐ Although performing his current duties very adequately, has no potential for further promotion.

☐ Displays abilities which may make him a suitable candidate for a job in the same grade but in a different discipline.

List Job(s) ....

Identified ....

☐ Has potential to be promoted should the opportunity occur.

List Job(s) ....

Identified ....

....

C. EMPLOYEE'S ASPIRATIONS Describe the employee's career aspirations, noting relevant details about interests, mobility, previous experience, etc.

D. DEVELOPMENT REPORT Describe the Training and/or Job Experience necessary to allow potential to be realised.

E. ACTION Taking into account the above *and* the likely future needs of the Company, what action should be taken in respect of this employee.

F. SIGNATURES

Head of Department : ....

Director : ....

T144a Sept. 1981

SELF ASSESSMENT PERFORMANCE REPORT (Front)

SECTION 1 MANAGEMENT BY OBJECTIVES	SECTION 2 JOB KNOWLEDGE	SECTION 3 QUALITY OF WORK	SECTION 4 INDUSTRY AND APPLICATION
This section must be completed for all staff in Grade 6 and above. For staff in Grades 5A and below this section need only be completed where objectives have been set. Except where special circumstances exist the overall Weighting to be applied to Section 1, Management by Objectives, will be 40%.	Consider here the theoretical, practical and/or technical knowledge possessed by the incumbent in relation to his present job.	Consider here the thoroughness, accuracy and reliability of the work done.	Consider here the volume of effective work the level of diligence, enthusiasm and persistent effort applied to the job.
Objectives significantly surpassed or achieved with considerable effort.	Has exceptionally wide and up-to-date knowledge of present job and related matters.	Quality of work is of a consistently high standard and reliability.	Wholehearted commitment, application and dedication to the tasks in hand. Extremely energetic and keen. High and effective work rate.
Objectives achieved with good effort or partially achieved with outstanding effort.	Has sound knowledge of job: well informed.	Quality of work is good and there are few occasions when accuracy, content and/or reliability can be questioned.	Hard working, keen and energetic, quick on uptake. Works well without prompting Above average work rate.
Objectives achieved with moderate effort or partially achieved with good effort .	Has sufficient knowledge to cope with job.	Can be relied upon to produce work which in terms of accuracy and reliability is satisfactory.	Generally works well but does not stand out as an exceptionally hard working and/or energetic person.
Objectives partially achieved with moderate effort.	Has limited knowledge and not too well informed.	Quality of work leaves something to be desired in accuracy, presentation and reliability. Can be careless.	Low output, easily baulked by minor setbacks and/or opposition. Inclined to be too easy going. Does sufficient to get by.
Little accomplished – little effort	Despite experience in the job has less knowledge than can be expected. Displays serious weaknesses and/or limitations in essential knowledge.	Quality of work cannot be relied on, prone to make repeat mistakes.	Lazy and/or lacking energy. Shows insufficient interest in the job. Neglects work.
New employee in Grade 6 and above, Objectives not set for this year.	Recently appointed and has incomplete Knowledge of Job.	Recently appointed and too early to judge Quality of Work.	Recently appointed and to early to judge Industry and Application.

.3

SEPT. 1981

Name : ____________________ Department : ____________________

SELF ASSESSMENT PERFORMANCE REPORT (Reverse)

SECTION 5 **INITIATIVE, INNOVATION AND JUDGEMENT** Consider here the ability to analyse problems and evaluate data objectively and form appropriate course of action. Consider also the ability to produce constructive ideas appropriate to his area of operation.	SECTION 6 **ATTITUDE, ADAPTABILITY AND EMOTIONAL MATURITY** Consider here the ability to meet and accept change, the need to work together towards common goals, the behaviour, attitude and manner towards subordinates, colleagues and seniors. Consider also the ability to deal with facts and situations in an objective and unemotional manner.	SECTION 7 **DECISION MAKING** Consider here the quality and promptness of decisions made, together with the acceptance of responsibility for those decisions.	SECTION 8 **LEADERSHIP, STAFF CONTROL COMMUNICATION AND DELEGATION** Consider here the ability and capacity to motivate, plan, delegate and to establish adequate controls, to organise, to communicate and to co-ordinate. Consider also man management ability.
Demonstrates sound judgement, based on clear common sense thinking and a well developed critical faculty. Not afraid to use initiative which is skilfully applied . Resourceful, confident and full of ideas.	Enthusiastic, sincere, loyal, co-operative and completely reliable in every way. Open minded to new ideas and concepts with the ability to deal with facts and situations calmly and in an emotionally mature manner. Nevertheless not afraid to speak his mind and defend his view forcefully when circumstances demand such an approach.	Prepared to make decisions promptly and takes care to try to make them correctly. Does not shirk the difficult decision but knows when to refer decision making process up the line. Accepts responsibility for his decisions.	Most capable leader, morale in department high. Inspires confidence. Effective and persuasive communicator both up and down. Prepared to delegate responsibility with corresponding authority and helps subordinates to improve and develop.
Good and well balanced judgement demonstrated in difficult situations. Uses initiative sensibly and generally has good ideas.	Conscientious employee who adapts well to new situations. Helpful and cheerful attitude. Emotionally balanced. Easy to work with. Can generally be counted on to express and defend his viewpoint.	Reaches sensible and prompt decisions about most matters in his area of responsibility. Likes to sound out seniors before announcing decisions.	Controls staff effectively, a good example and influence and a good leader. Demonstrates a clear ability to direct others to reach common goals. Delegates and communicates well.
Judgement is sometimes uncertain. Sometimes hesitates to take initiative. Some ideas but really not an innovator.	Generally reliable and co-operative. Copes adequately with most work and people situations. Works reasonably well with most people.	Occasionally cannot see wood for trees and refers too many items up the line for decision. Reluctant to accept responsibility for decisions. Tends to take too long in reaching decisions. Plays for safety.	Generally handles staff well but is happier as a team member rather than a leader. Tries hard to communicate and delegate effectively.
Generally avoids the unusual or new situation unless pushed. Normally not prepared to take the initiative. Judgement can be called into question. Often takes the easy way out.	Seldom seen to put himself out. Occasionally loses sense of proportion and creates situation of friction and tension.	Finds considerable difficulty in making sound decisions on the simplest of subjects.	Not always in complete control of section or department. Has difficulty in controlling and leading. Finds delegation difficult.
Woolly thinker lacking initiative, and balanced judgement with little or no self confidence, and no ideas.	Often unco-operative with a blinkered approach to any new ideas. Given to getting things out of proportion.	Not prepared to make decisions, refers all items up the line.	Has little control over staff, too easy going. Does not inspire confidence. Little or no interest shown in developing subordinates. Communication skills leave much to be desired.
Recently appointed and too early to judge Initiative, Innovation and Judgement.	Recently appointed and too early to judge Attitude, Adaptability and Emotional Maturity.	Recently appointed and too early to judge Decision Making.	Recently appointed and too early to judge Leadership, Staff Control, Communication and Delegation.

Example E

The format is completely different from the previous example, although used in another division of the same multinational organization. The focus of the review is on improvement and development and is quite separate from the bonus award system, although obviously complimentary. All monthly paid employees are included in the review system.

In contrast to the tightly quantified structure of Example D, the style is free narrative with brief guidelines outlining the main topics for consideration. The document is a record of the review discussion and is seen and signed by the jobholder. The review discussion is of prime importance to the system and appraisal training workshops have been a regular feature for the past five years (managers from Example D are included in these). The individual jobholder is encouraged to prepare an aide-memoire for the discussion.

A separate personal and career development review is optional.

PERFORMANCE IMPROVEMENT REVIEW RECORD	Name:	Department:
	Title/Grade:	Date:

This written record should be divided into sections:

Section 1: Achievement should be used to describe the extent to which the individual member of staff has achieved his/her work objectives and/or successfully carried out the required range of tasks during the appraisal year.

Section 2: Individual Performance Characteristics should be used to highlight those aspects of performance which have significantly helped or hindered the individual in achieving his/her objectives. Such aspects might include reference to technical ability or knowledge; creativity; planning ability; communication/interaction ability; application and motivation; and leadership or managerial ability.

Section 3: Goals should be used to record any agreed changes in job objectives, and any performance improvement goals, specifying where appropriate what assistance will be given to the individual to achieve these objectives and goals, e.g. training plan for next year.

Section 4: Personal & Career Development Review; should be used to record whether or not a separate P&CDR is required, and if so, the planned date. If a separate P&CDR is not required any discussion relevant to longer term issues such as career aspirations, potential career opportunities or alternative career pathways should be recorded.

Reviewer ....

Reviewer's Manager ....

Staff Member ....

T84

Example F

This format is also in a free narrative style and is an example of a combined self and supervisory assessment. The approach is results-oriented and includes a separate list of major goals and achievement plans. There are no overall performance gradings or ratings.

This scheme has been used in a manufacturing organization for the past five years by management, professional and technical employees. A slightly modified version - more controlled narrative - is used for the salesforce. A development plan is included, with dated and named responsibility for action. The jobholder retains a copy of the complete document.

Training workshops are held for all those involved in the review system, including those with no supervisory responsibilities.

CONFIDENTIAL

PERFORMANCE & DEVELOPMENT REVIEW FORM

APPRAISEE'S NAME:	PERIOD COVERED BY
POSITION:	ACCOMPLISHMENT
APPRAISER'S NAME:	SUMMARY
POSITION:	(YEAR) ....

1. ACCOMPLISHMENT SUMMARY

INSTRUCTIONS TO THE APPRAISEE:

1. As the appraisee, it is your responsibility to complete this section. It will form the basis for a performance review and development planning discussion with your manager. Please read 'A Guide to the Managerial Performance Appraisal System' before completing.
2. If you prepared formal goals for the current year, complete the 'Performance' section of each goals form and attach them to this form. In the space below, summarise any other important accomplishments not covered by the goals forms. If you did not prepare formal goals for the current year, list your major duties in the space below. After each, report briefly on what you accomplished in respect to these duties. Include any extra accomplishments or special objectives set.
3. Upon completion of this section, please hand this form to your appraising manager and arrange a meeting to discuss the information.
4. Attach extra sheets as appropriate.

COMPLETED BY (SIGNED): ....

DATE: ....

2. PERFORMANCE SUMMARY

INSTRUCTIONS TO THE APPRAISER:

1. Review the Accomplishment Summary.
2. Meet with the appraisee to discuss his/her performance for the year in relation to job responsibilities, goals and expectations. This is an opportunity to clarify job responsibilities, to agree on additional steps that remain to be taken to fulfill requirements and recognise strong performance. Career goals should also be discussed, along with measures to improve effectiveness or develop for the future. It may be useful to prepare notes for the discussion.
3. Summarise your discussion with the appraisee in the space below. Include comments on performance versus goals and/or job responsibilities.
4. Summarise your discussion on development plans on page 4.
5. Attach extra sheets as appropriate.

COMPLETED BY (SIGNED): ....

DATE: ....

3. DEVELOPMENT PLAN

Please record the activities planned to assist in improving the appraisee's effectiveness or likelihood for advancement. This may include special projects, change in responsibilities, further education or training.

DEVELOPMENT ACTIVITIES

	COMPLETION DATE & RESPONSIBILITY FOR ENSURING ACTION TAKEN:
A. ON THE JOB	
B. TRAINING/EDUCATION	

COMPLETED BY (SIGNED): .... DATE: ....

REVIEWED BY (SIGNED- NEXT LEVEL): .... DATE: ....

THE PERFORMANCE & DEVELOPMENT DISCUSSION TOOK PLACE ON: ....

TIME SPENT: ....

A COPY WAS GIVEN TO THE APPRAISEE ON: ....

GOALS REPORT FOR PERIOD:

NAME: POSITION: GOAL NO. OF

602 C23

GOAL TITLE:

MAJOR ACTION STEPS PLANNED	ANTICIPATED COMPLETION DATES	PERFORMANCE REVIEW (UP TO ________ (DATE))

1984 ANNUAL APPRAISAL

TERRITORY SALESMEN

Name ....

Reporting to ....

(Male gender is used throughout for convenience only)

1. ACCOMPLISHMENT SUMMARY

The annual appraisal is an opportunity to discuss your performance over the year and to set targets for the coming year. In order to prepare for your appraisal interview , it will be useful to consider the questions below and answer them in the spaces provided. State ' facts ' where appropriate.

Q. **How have you performed against campaign targets ?**

A.

Q. **How effective is your call coverage and journey planning ?**

A.

Q. **How many new accounts have you opened this year ?**

A.

Q. **What do you consider to be your strengths ?**

A.

Q. What areas of your on - the - job performance do you feel I can help to improve ?

A.

Q. What action do you think the Company can take to make your operation more effective ?

A.

Q. Do you consider yourself to be an effective Territory manager ? Why ?

A.

Q. What are your short and long - term career objectives ?

A.

\- - - - - - - -

Please enter any additional achievements / comments below :

2. PERFORMANCE SUMMARY

(To be completed by Area Sales Manager at end of interview)

3. DEVELOPMENT PLAN

Completion date and responsibility for action .

ON THE JOB :

LONG - TERM :

The performance and development discussion took place on ---------- Time spent -------

Signed ----------------	Signed ----------------	Signed ----------------
(Territory Salesman)	(Area Sales Manager)	(Regional Sales Manager)
Date ----------------	Date ----------------	Date ----------------

TARGETS REPORT FOR PERIOD :

NAME : **POSITION :** **TARGET NO. OF**

TARGET TITLE

MAJOR ACTION STEPS PLANNED	ANTICIPATED COMPLETION DATES	PERFORMANCE REVIEW (UP TO . . . .(DATE))

Example G

This results-oriented scheme has been in use for just one year, the previous scheme having lapsed some years ago. The present system was introduced after a two year period of discussion, development and training. At the time of the survey it was being piloted among the senior grades of employee for one review period. The intention was to introduce it for the remaining employees for the following review period if the results of the pilot were favourable. A post-review audit revealed that the approach had been very well accepted by both jobholders and managers. Some minor improvements were needed before the launch of the final phase in time for the next review period.

Essentially the emphasis is on key task areas and performance improvement. The jobholder is encouraged to fully participate in setting targets and objectives, a 'self-assessment' form on similar lines to the review document being provided. The performance record is narrative in style and there is no overall performance summary or rating.

Form B

Private and Confidential Review Year........................

Performance Review Record Form

Name .... Department/Branch ....

Job Title .... Job Grade .... Staff No. ....

Date of appointment to present position ....

Professional qualifications (including degrees) ....

....

....

The purpose of this form is to review past performance, to set new targets and to improve the job holder's performance. Prior to the review you should study the individual's job and previous review record forms so that your attention is focused on the targets that he/she has been trying to achieve.

1. Targets under review

List Agreed Targets	*Target Completion Date*	*Comments on Attainment against Targets* (show degree of success including the extent of any over or under achievement)

Name .... Review Year........................

Peformance Review Record Form

2. Future Targets

This section should be used to set targets for next year concentrating on Key Result Areas. Performance levels for each target should be defined in measurable terms.

List Agreed Targets	*Target Completion Date*	*Levels of Performance*

Review Year........................

Performance Review Record Form

Name .... Department/Branch ....

Job Title .... Job Grade .... Staff No. ....

Date of appointment to present position ....

Professional qualifications (including degrees) ....

....

....

3. (i) Action taken to improve performance

Reviewer should check that the measures contained in 3 (ii) the previous year were actioned.

3. (ii) Action needed to improve performance

Reviewer should consider what needs to be done to assist job holder in meeting new targets. What is required in the way of experience and training?

4. Any other relevant points and general comments

5. Prepared by ....(Printed Name)

Signed ....

Job Title ....

Date ....

Signed by the job holder ....

Date ....

Seen by Executive Head ....

CS 2769/0
11-84

Form A

Confidential to Job Holder

Review Year........................

Performance Review – Self Assessment

Name ....

Please note that your annual review has been arranged for (date) ....

at .... am/pm with .... in ....

The purpose of this more formal discussion with your Manager or Supervisor is to review your performance over the year against your agreed targets; to consider the setting of new targets; and to identify ways in which your performance can be improved.

Arising from the discussion any training needs you may have should be identified.

In preparation please carefully consider the headings mentioned which are basic to this discussion. The form is simply a guide to help you prepare for useful discussion during your interview. You should complete the form which can be used for reference during the discussion if you wish. This form is merely a guide to your own thinking. It does not have to be shown to anyone. After the discussion it is for you to keep or destroy if you wish.

The value of the interview to you will depend chiefly on what you contribute to it. You may discuss any matters which in your opinion affect performance and productivity in your present job or may have a bearing on your future career.

1. **List targets previously agreed**	2. **What progress have you made towards meeting each of these targets?**

3. What targets do you consider appropriate for the next year?

4. Are there any ways whereby your effectiveness in achieving your targets could be enhanced? Do you need more knowledge of particular matters?

5. Do you foresee any developments in your areas of accountability over the next year which could affect the achievement of future targets and therefore should be discussed?

6. Have you any other observations?

Example H

This results-oriented scheme was introduced three years ago for management and professional employees in a large multi-divisional organization. Surveys were carried out one and two years after its introduction to monitor impact, progress and improvements. Appraisal training workshops have been an important part of the pre- and post-introduction period. Jobholders are encouraged to prepare for the review discussion, using a blank review form.

The format is mainly free narrative, concentrating on agreed, achieved and future objectives, training needs and self-development. The jobholder's own views and wishes form a major section of the review document. An overall performance rating and estimates of potential and promotion prospects are required for the summary page, a copy of which is placed on record. The assessor retains the complete original record but the jobholder keeps a copy.

CONFIDENTIAL

Performance Review

Name

Date of Birth — Date of Appointment to post

Qualifications

Title of post held — Grade

Region/Business

Department — Year

Courses attended during past 3 years

Date of last career review (if any)

SUMMARY Performance rating

1 ☐ Exceptional
2 ☐ Excellent
3 ☐ Competent
4 ☐ Below standard
5 ☐ Unsatisfactory

Before completing these boxes the guidance notes should be read carefully for explanation of terms.

Should the job-holder be considered for a change of job within the next 12 months?

On Promotion ☐ Yes ☐ No — For Other Reasons ☐ Yes ☐ No

Is assistance required in meeting the training/education needs of the job-holder?

☐ YES ☐ NO

The job-holder is willing/not willing for the complete document to be made available for selection purposes.

For how many promotions has the job-holder potential?

A ☐ 5+ B ☐ 3/4 C ☐ 1/2 D ☐ – probably no more promotions

A detailed career review is necessary

☐ YES ☐ NO

Signature of assessor

Name — Signature

Post — Date

Counter-signature

I am satisfied that the review has been carried out and discussed conscientiously.
I agree the performance rating or I have amended it after discussion with the assessor.

Comments

Name — Signature

Post — Date

1 Review of performance

1.1 What objectives were agreed against which success in the job is to be judged?

1.2 Comment on the extent of achievement of the above objectives.

2 Future performance and training needs

2.1 How can the job-holder improve his or her performance by personal action?

2.2 What management action, counselling, training or work experience is necessary to enable the job-holder to improve his or her performance in the post?

3 Objectives for next 12 months

What objectives are agreed for the next twelve months?

4 Job-holder's views

I have discussed the foregoing review with the assessor and have the following comments to make:

I am willing/not willing for the information contained in sections 1 to 4 of this document to be made available for selection purposes should I apply for another post.

Signed Date

SUMMARY OF GUIDELINES

(To be read in conjunction with Performance Review Guide)

Staff to be reviewed

The performance of all senior managers and management staff will be reviewed. For some posts in management ranges 1 and 2 which have little managerial content it may not be appropriate to complete sections 1 to 4. Assessors will require their manager's approval for this. In all cases the Summary on the front page must be completed by the assessor and counter-signature obtained.

Procedure

The objectives for the past year (1.1) should be completed by the assessor first. The assessor will normally be the job-holder's immediate superior. If the job-holder has been in the post for less than 3-4 months the previous employer should be asked to complete Section 1 and the summary. It may be helpful for the job-holder as well as the assessor to draft Sections 1.2, 2 and 3 independently, prior to the meeting.

Assessors should then discuss job-holders performance with them, covering the successes of the year as well as the shortcomings, and agree a course of action for both of them which is then used to complete Sections 1.2, 2 and 3.

The assessor should then complete the Summary on the front page. The expression of opinion about potential for promotion will be taken into account in considering whether a formal career review is necessary.

Job-holders should then complete Section 4 to indicate their agreement or any views they want to express which the assessor has not recorded in Sections 1 or 2. If necessary, job-holders must be given time to reflect and a second meeting may be necessary.

Only the front page will be copied, to be used for personnel purposes including the award of merit payments. It is therefore essential that the assessor keeps the original and ensures that required action is pursued. The job-holder will be given a personal copy.

Counter-Signature

The form will then be sent to the nominated counter-signatory, who will be the assessor's manager, or someone delegated by him or her who knows the requirements of the job well. Any remarks which contradict those of assessors should be discussed with them and in turn with the job-holder

Example I

This is another example of a results-oriented scheme for management and professional employees, used in a European-based division of a very large multinational organization, where all personnel systems are centrally designed.

The review documentation is in two parts. One part is the performance discussion summary in which equal emphasis is given to major job objectives and employee-centred topics such as employee development plans, self-development, career aspirations and other personal concerns and interests. Factors influencing both these main areas are taken into consideration. The jobholder is expected to participate fully and preparation guidelines are provided. The discussion summary contains the overall performance rating and is signed by the jobholder. The second document is not seen by the jobholder and contains the performance review summary and overall rating, an estimate of potential by the second level reviewer and a detailed individual management development plan. The system is pay-related and the main problem is the skewing of the overall rating towards the higher ratings. This is one area which will be considered when the system is next revised, possibly substituting a descriptive overall performance evaluation.

REVISED – JAN. 1983
CONFIDENTIAL
PDS - 83

PERFORMANCE DISCUSSION SUMMARY

(PROFESSIONAL & MANAGEMENT EMPLOYEES)

Name ______________________ Position title ______________________

Department ______________ Location ______________ Date ______________

A. ANALYSIS OF PERFORMANCE

1. Major results expected during the appraisal period

2. Degree to which results were accomplished
   (a) Results achieved

   (b) Results not achieved

3. Factors (situational or personal) which helped or hindered accomplishment of results

B. OVERALL EVALUATION OF PERFORMANCE

C. OBJECTIVES FOR NEXT APPRAISAL PERIOD

1. What are the major results to be accomplished during the next period?

2. What specific difficulties are anticipated? How will they be overcome?

D. EMPLOYEE IMPROVEMENT/DEVELOPMENT

1. Specific programs which have been worked out with the employee

2. Employee's aspirations
   (a) Preferred type of work ____________________

   (b) Personal limitations ____________________
   (Restriction on travel, relocation, type of work, etc.)

   (c) Language skills ____________________
   (Additional competence since last discussion)

   (d) Other ____________________
   (Interest in specific locations or special types of assignment)

3. Employee retirement plans (if relevant, and employee wishes to discuss)

E. OTHER IMPORTANT TOPICS DISCUSSED

Employee concerns, interests, comments on work climate, etc.

F. SIGNIFICANT COMMENTS BEYOND THOSE COVERED IN FOREGOING ITEMS

(Other employee aptitudes, studies, professional activities, etc.)

IF THERE IS INSUFFICIENT SPACE UNDER ANY HEADING, WRITE ADDITIONAL COMMENTS HERE

Date of discussion ______________________

Employee signature ______________________

Name, title and signature of appraiser ______________________

Name, title and signature of the next higher supervisor ______________________

REVISED – JAN. 1983
CONFIDENTIAL
EAS-83

EMPLOYEE APPRAISAL SUMMARY
(PROFESSIONAL & MANAGEMENT EMPLOYEES)

Department ______________ Location ______________ Date ______________

NAME ______________ Nationality ______________ Present position ______________ SSGL ______

Birth date ______________ A.S.D. ______________ Date assigned present SSGL ______________ Date assigned present position ______________

EDUCATION
(Highest qualification) Discipline ______________ Degree (etc.) ______________
Language capability (1 = mother tongue or equivalent; 2 = adequate for business proficiency)

E	F	G	D	I	Sp	Sw	Other(s)

Comments: ______________
____

CURRENT PERFORMANCE: O ☐ V ☐ G ☐ S ☐ U ☐
OR, IF IN JOB LESS THAN 3 MONTHS, RATE OF ADJUSTMENT IS: Fast ☐ Normal ☐ Slow ☐

PERFORMANCE

A. PRESENT ASSIGNMENT

1. ACCOMPLISHMENT (Summarise significant results achieved during past period)

2. CONTRIBUTING FACTORS (Identify those characteristics or factors which significantly contributed to achievement of results; and those which will benefit most from further development).

CONTRIBUTING TO ACCOMPLISHMENT

BENEFITING FROM DEVELOPMENT
(or detracting from accomplishment)

Name and Title of appraiser ______________

POTENTIAL

B. DEGREE OF POTENTIAL (To be completed by higher line management)

1. POTENTIAL ESTIMATE (Estimate employee's potential for Supervisory/Management (not professional progression) advancement within next 10 years)

Supervisory/Managerial

☐ – A	Can advance more than 2 full SSGL
☐ – B	Can advance 1½ to 2 full SSGL
☐ – C	Can advance up to & including 1 full SSGL
☐ – D	Advancement unlikely

Indicate if in Professional Progression ☐

State basic reasons to support this estimate:

If appropriate, identify specific positions to which employee could advance.

2. ASSESSMENT OF EMPLOYEE CAREER ASPIRATIONS	REALISTIC	UNREALISTIC
(a) Next one or two positions desired ____________	☐	☐
____________	☐	☐
(b) Long range career objective ____________	☐	☐
(c) Preferred type of work ____________	☐	☐

C. If qualified for positions in other than present field, company or country, state why(employee's interests, aptitudes — or relate to significant contributions).

DEVELOPMENT

D. EMPLOYEE DEVELOPMENT PLANS

MANAGEMENT ASSESSMENT OF DEVELOPMENT NEEDED OR DESIRABLE

(A) Training to maintain or strengthen performance in present position or to prepare for next position.

Principal skills or attributes to benefit from training (See Sect A2)	Programme	To be completed Q./Yr.
1. ______	______	______
2. ______	______	______
3. ______	______	______
4. ______	______	______

(B) Assignments to prepare employee for potential shown in Section B1. (Show all assignments anticipated for next three years.)

Position	Purpose	Timing Q./Yr.
Within 12 months ______	______	______
1-3 years ______	______	______
______	______	______

______

______

Names and Titles of others completing this appraisal

P-77

TO :

FROM :

PREPARATION SHEET FOR ANNUAL PERFORMANCE DISCUSSION

INTRODUCTION

The annual performance discussion provides an opportunity to take time to analyze what the job expect of us and how well we are meeting those expectations. Thoughtful analysis will suggest areas for improvement or growth to help us better realize our realistic aspirations for the future. It also provides a chance for management to learn how we all can maintain and improve a good working climate.

I want you to participate, not just to listen. To help us prepare for a meaningful discussion, you should thoughtfully review each of the following items. Rough notes are sufficient. Since I will be considering the same points, our respective responses can provide a common agenda for the performance discussion. Our objective is to reach common understanding.

After the discussion, I will document it on a Performance Discussion Summary form for higher management review.

The following questions follow a sequence to help us to organize our thoughts, analyze them, discover what we have learned from this past year's experiences and to plan how to use what we have learned. You need not answer every supplementary question that follows each item, below. They are simply intended to explain further what each item means.

ANALYSIS OF PERFORMANCE

1. Major results expected

   What significant expected results were agreed between us at the last performance discussion ? What additional or alternative results were agreed since that discussion ?

2. Degree to which results were accomplished

   (a) Results achieved

   What were your major accomplishments this past year ?
   What accomplishments demonstrated particular strengths ? What parts of your job did you do the best ? What parts of your job required special skill or knowledge ? What impact did your results have ?

   (b) Results not achieved

   What objectives were not reached ? Why ? Which of them suggest opportunities for improvement ?

3. Factors which helped or hindered accomplishment of results

   What helped you accomplish what you did ? What sorts of things do you have going for you that help you get things done ? (Persistence, analytical skill, specialized knowledge, past experience, etc). Or, what sorts of things prevented you from accomplishing some parts of your job as well as you accomplished other parts of it ? Did you fully understand what the job expected of you ? Did you and I agree on priorities of assignments ? Did you feel "on top" of all parts of your job ? What parts took the most effort or time ? How much help did you need to get things done ? Were they any factors affecting accomplishments over which you had no control ?

.../

Has anything concerning your job changed significantly during the past year ? If so, what ? In what ways did you improve or further develop your capabilities ? What new knowledge, skill, or experience did you gain ?

OBJECTIVES FOR NEXT APPRAISAL PERIOD

1. Major results to be accomplished

   What major results need to be accomplished in the coming year ? What priorities do you assign them ? What should be the basis for evaluating your performance ? (Throughout the appraisal period, you and I will review these goals and your progress toward them).

2. Difficulties anticipated

   Are any of the trouble areas encountered during the last period likely to recur ? Can you anticipate new factors which might pose barriers to accomplishments ? If so, what can we do to minimize them ?

EMPLOYEE IMPROVEMENT/DEVELOPMENT

1. Specific Programs

   What, if anything, should you or we do to improve accomplishment of results ? (What additional knowledge, skill, experiences, or formal training would help ? How can this be built into your present assignment ?). What can we do in your present assignment to help you enhance your value to yourself and to the company ?

2. Career Aspirations

   What are your career objectives in terms of activities, functions, specific jobs ? Does your job challenge you ? What reasonable actions, near term, would enhance chances for realization ? How do you feel about your present job ? Does it provide opportunity to get additional knowledge, skill, and experience ? What kinds of work do you like ? What kinds of assignments would you prefer to avoid ? (How do you feel about moving from your present geographical location ?).

3. Retirement Plans (if relevant)

   Do you want to talk about your plans for retirement ? Do you wish to retire before the mandatory age ? locally ? or at some other location ?

OTHER IMPORTANT TOPICS

What other significant items should we discuss ? What other aspects of the job do you want to talk about ? How do you feel about the work climate surrounding your job ? Are there any specific interests, problems or concerns you would like to discuss ?

OTHER SIGNIFICANT COMMENTS

Do you have any particular skills or experience not being used in your present assignment ? Are there any off-the-job studies, activities, professional association responsibilities, etc., which should be noted.

Are there any other items not specified above which you feel need to be discussed ?

March 1977

Example J

This scheme is in use in a medium-sized manufacturing organization and applies to all grades of employee, including the hourly paid. It was introduced about two years ago to replace a salary-linked system, based on ratings. The emphasis of the present scheme is on major objectives and the improvement and development of performance. The jobholder is encouraged to participate in the review discussion and a preparation form is provided, which is completed and given to the reviewer two weeks prior to the discussion. This does not apply to the junior clerical grades or hourly-paid employees.

There are three similar review forms in use for the various grades of employee. The one used for secretarial, clerical and administrative staff is an interesting example of the application of a results-oriented approach for this level of employee. The format used for hourly-paid employees is simpler but, although including comments on attendance and teamwork, still has an objective slant.

Performance Appraisal

MANAGERIAL

TECHNICAL &

PROFESSIONAL

STAFF

NAME & INITIALS:	JOB TITLE:

EMPLOYMENT DATE:	LENGTH OF SERVICE IN CURRENT POSITION:

DEPARTMENT/DIVISION:	ZONE NUMBER:	PLACE AND DATE OF APPRAISAL DISCUSSION:

PREPARED BY: (Name and Signature)	APPROVED BY: (Name and Signature)

PERFORMANCE REVIEW

RESULTS: (High priority goals/objectives. A summary of actual achievements since the last performance review.)

List individuals agreed goals/objectives over the review period. Assess achievements against specific goals, quoting examples and quantifying results whenever possible.

List any additional areas in which the individual has shown significant performance over the appraisal period.

PERFORMANCE SUMMARY

Summarise overall performance against objectives for the prior year.

Comment of Individual to Appraisal Review

Signature..Date..................

Action by Human Resources Dept

Signature..Date..................

DEVELOPMENT PLANS

Describe specific steps to improve the individual within the current job that can build on strengths and improve shortcomings. Indicate any Career Development plans if appropriate. (A copy of the Development Plans should be given to the employee)

FUTURE OBJECTIVES

Define in specific measurable terms, with target date for completion, the agreed high priority goals/objectives for the next appraisal period. Normally five or six major objectives should be sufficient. (A copy of the Future Objectives should be handed to the employee)

Performance Appraisal

CLERICAL

SECRETARIAL &

ADMINISTRATIVE STAFF

NAME & INITIALS:	JOB TITLE:

EMPLOYMENT DATE:	LENGTH OF SERVICE IN CURRENT POSITION:

DEPARTMENT/DIVISION:	PLACE, TIME, AND DATE OF APPOINTMENT.

PREPARED BY:	APPROVED BY:

JOB OBJECTIVES	COMMENTS ON ATTAINMENT	FUTURE JOB OBJECTIVES
List job objectives and standards of performance required in terms of quality, quantity, deadlines etc.	Against each objective comment on how effective the employee was in meeting requirements. Where possible, quote specific examples.	Note any specific tasks/objectives/activities - that need to be highlighted/achieved over the next 12 months. List standards required and deadlines to be met.

ADDITIONAL SIGNIFICANT RESULTS.

PERFORMANCE SUMMARY.

Summarise overall performance against objectives for the prior year.

FURTHER DEVELOPMENT

List what proposed action is necessary to develop the employee or to overcome any performance weaknesses. Indicate a time scale for completion and the person responsible.

RESPONSE OF THE INDIVIDUAL TO THE APPRAISAL REVIEW.

Signature.. Date.......................

PERFORMANCE APPRAISAL

NAME AND INITIALS	JOB TITLE

EMPLOYMENT DATE	LENGTH OF SERVICE IN CURRENT POSITION

Prepared by (Name & Signature)	Approved by (Name & Signature)
Supervisor	Manager

Performance Review

Comment on the employee's performance over the last 12 months against Job Standard.

Other Significant Achievments

List any other additional areas in which the employee has shown significant achievements during the review period.

Attendance/Lateness

Comment on the employee's Attendance Record during the review period.

Teamwork

How well does the employee play a part in the Team.

Training/Development

Describe any specific steps to improve the employee's performance and any personal ambitions the employee may have for the future.

Future Performance

List any points or objectives the employee needs to achieve to maintain or improve performance over the next 12 months.

Comment of individual

Employee's comment on Appraisal Review.

Signature ____________________ Date ____________________

Preparation for Appraisal

NAME:	JOB TITLE:

LOCATION/DEPARTMENT/DIVISION/ZONE NUMBER:

APPRAISERS NAME:	DATE/TIME/LOCATION OF APPRAISAL:

Dear

It is policy to review the performance and development of every employee on a regular basis, culminating with an overall review at an annual Appraisal Interview.

The purpose of the interview is to assist you in developing your abilities, increasing your job satisfaction and preparing for future objectives.

I have arranged for us to meet at the place and time indicated above and look forward to this as an opportunity to plan for the future.

The value of the interview depends very much on your contribution and you are invited to discuss any subjects which, in your opinion, are related to your job satisfaction, productivity or career development.

The purpose of the meeting is not to discuss salary, this will be dealt with on another occasion.

In order to help us both prepare for the interview I would be grateful if you could complete the following form and return it to me at least two weeks before the appraisal.

At the interview the form will be given back to you and you may use it for reference (although you need not strictly adhere to it). After the interview you may keep it or give it to your Manager for filing with your personal records

I look forward to our discussion.

Signed.................................

Title..................................

1. List your agreed objectives for the prior year and describe your performance against them. Describe any difficulties you may have had and how you overcame them.

2. What other significant accomplishments did you achieve in the past year?

3. Does your job fully utilise your accomplishments or abilities? If not, how could your skills be used more fully?

4. Which areas in your job performance do you feel could be improved with the help of either yourself or your Manager? Please state the particular action to be taken and by whom.

5. Do you find any aspect of your job unsatisfactory? If so, how could the situation be improved?

6. What job objectives would you like to achieve in the next appraisal year?

7. Are there any areas in your job or the Company about which you would like more information, either from your Manager or from anyone else?

8. How do you see your career developing over the next four years? Would you require any special training or education to achieve this? Are there any areas within, or outside of your own position/department that particularly interest you and why is that so?

9. Have you any suggestions that could help to make a more satisfactory company in which to work for yourself or other employees?

10. Use this space if you have any other comments not covered by the questions above.

Example K

This scheme has recently been revised and is in use in a very large multinational organization which has undergone a major development programme. The revision and development of the performance review system was accompanied by intensive discussions, education and training programmes over the period of a year. The salary-link has been removed.

The emphasis of the scheme is on key task areas and objective setting and the identification of training needs for the current job. All grades of employee are included and employee participation in the review is encouraged. Preparation notes are provided for the job-holder which also include a section for post-review comments. Although the format of the three review forms varies, there is a strong orientation towards objectives and job components. An overall performance rating and estimate of possible potential is required for all grades of employee.

This form should be completed in accordance with the Booklet *"Performance Review and Appraisal – A Guide for Managers"*, **copies of which are available from the Personnel Department. Following completion, the appraisal form should be returned to the Director of Personnel.**

CONFIDENTIAL

Performance Review & Appraisal

For Staff in Level 4 (or equivalent) and above. The form may also be used for Staff in Level 5 (or equivalent) where appropriate.

Period under review

Name and initials

Date of Birth | Dept./Location

Grade/Level | Job Grade/Level (if different)

Present Post

Head Office Job Number | Date of Appointment to Post

1. Objective for Coming Year

Direction, principal thrust, profit responsibility:

Resources to be employed:
(Indication of scope of job in terms of people, capital, budgets and other resources)

2. Targets for the Coming Year *(List in order of importance)*

Results to be achieved	Target level of achievement
1.	
2.	
3.	
4.	
5.	

ASSUMPTIONS

3. Summary of Performance Appraisal

Comments *(Identify any individual strengths or problems which influenced achievement of the targets and*

Joint Accountability	Initials	Analysis of Results and action to be taken (include reasons for over- or under- achievement)	Initials

(state target to which they refer)

general performance)	Overall rating
	1. Achievements outstanding ☐ 2. Achievements exceeded the requirements of the job ☐ 3. Achieved the requirements of the job ☐ 4. Some aspects of achievement below requirements ☐ 5. Performance unacceptable at this level ☐

Signature of Appraisee____________________ Date____________________

4. Training required for current position

5. Estimate of possible potential

a) What sort of role? b) At what level? c) In what time frame?	d) Development required for long term growth/potential

6. Appraiser's Comments

Signature *Name in Capitals* *Date*

7. Reviewer's Comments

Signature *Name in Capitals* *Date*

Business Head/Head of Division's initials:

FORM PRA/1/84
REPRO No: 160a

REFER TO NOTES FOR GUIDANCE BEFORE COMPLETING

CONFIDENTIAL

Executive Staff Appraisal

– For Staff in U.K. Level 7A/7B and above, and F1 Staff, not covered by '*Performance Review and Appraisal*'.

Period under review

Name and initials

Date of birth

Dept./Location

Present Post

Head Office Job Number | Date of Appointment to post

Level

Acting Level, if any | Date from | to

Following completion, the appraisal form should be returned to the Director of Personnel

Part 1A Performance Assessment

Performance Rating Scale

1. Performance outstanding
2. Performance exceeded requirements of job
3. Performed requirements of job
4. Some aspects of performance below requirements
5. Performance unacceptable at this level

Indicate the performance rating attained by putting a tick in the appropriate box against each job component listed and specify the overall rating in Part 1C.

Job components	Ratings					Comments
	1	**2**	**3**	**4**	**5**	

Part 1 B Key Tasks

Key tasks (to be agreed at commencement of financial year)	Achievements (to be agreed at conclusion of financial year)	Comments

Part 1 C Overall Performance Rating

1	2	3	4	5
☐	☐	☐	☐	☐

(See rating scale on previous page)

Part 2 Review

(a) When results have exceeded those which are required, what is it that he/she does to achieve this?

(b) Where results do not meet all the requirements which parts of the job should be tackled better?

(c) Action to be taken by Appraiser

(d) Action to be taken by Appraisee

Part 3 Training Requirements for Current Position

Signature of Appraisee ______________________ Date ______________________

Comments of Development & Training Manager

Signature of DTM ______________________ Date ______________________

Name in Block Capitals ______________________

Part 4 Estimate of Possible Potential

a) What sort of role?

b) At what level?

c) In what time frame?

d) Development required for longterm growth/potential

Signature of Appraiser ______________________ Date ______________________

Name in Block Capitals ______________________

Part 5 Comments of Reviewer

Signature of Reviewer ______________________ Date ______________________

Name in Block Capitals ______________________

Business Head/Head of Division's Initials: ______________________

REFER TO NOTES FOR GUIDANCE BEFORE COMPLETING

CONFIDENTIAL

Non-Executive Staff Appraisal

- For Staff in UK Level 8 and below.

Period under review

Name and initials

Date of birth

Dept./Location

Present Post

Head Office
Job Number — Date of Appointment to post

Level

Acting Level, if any — Date from — to

Following completion, the appraisal form should be returned to the Director of Personnel

Section A **Job Performance**

1. Assessment of the factors listed below should be based on results achieved against job standards. Indicate specifically particular strengths and weaknesses.

Job Components	Assessment
Regular Tasks 'One-off' Tasks	

General Factors	Comments
Job knowledge Work output (quantity) Work quality Job interest/enthusiasm Initiative	

2. Overall Performance Rating

☐ Performance outstanding

☐ Performance exceeded requirements of Job

☐ Performed requirements of Job

☐ Some aspects of performance below requirements

☐ Performance unacceptable

The rating chosen must be supported by comments above.

Section B **Training**

1. Training or action recommended to assist performance in current job

2. Further training and development recommendations

Signature of Appraisee

________________________ Date ____________________

Comments of Development and Training Manager

Signature of DTM ________________________ Name in Block Capitals ____________________

Date ____________________

Section C **Potential**

1. At present he/she seems: ready for promotion ☐
to have promotion potential ☐
to have reached potential ☐

2. What position or area of work do you recommend for next move for a) personal development and b) promotion? (include timescale). Indicate job holder's aspirations.

Signature of Appraiser ______________________ Date ______________________

Name in Block Capitals ______________________

Section D **Comments of Reviewer**

Signature of Reviewer ______________________ Date ______________________

Name in Block Capitals ______________________

Business Head/Head of Division's Initials: ______________________

REPRO No: 305

Preparation Notes for Executive Staff Appraisal

As part of its programme of staff development, the Company requires all members of the staff to be appraised annually by their manager.

A discussion of this kind can be of benefit to both you and the Company and you should try to take full advantage of it by so preparing for it as to ensure that it is as useful and constructive as possible.

The way to do this is to ask yourself a number of questions about your job, such as:-

What particular difficulties have I faced in my present job?

What action can be taken by my manager or myself to improve my performance?

These and other questions are given in Part 1 of these notes for you to answer. By considering such questions and trying to answer them you will be better equipped for the discussion with your manager.

Part 2 has been included to enable you to consider appropriate objectives for the coming year. These will then be discussed during the interview and once a set of tasks has been agreed these will be recorded in Part 1 B of the Appraisal. At the end of the period for which key tasks have been agreed your manager will be able to take into account your performance against these tasks when assessing your overall rating. Part 1 B of the Appraisal Form will therefore need to be covered in two separate discussions:-

i.e. a) review of performance against previously agreed tasks. This would form part of the main appraisal interview.

b) A separate discussion to agree key tasks for the forthcoming year.

If, as a result of the interview, there are any points which you wish to record, either concerning the period under review, or with a view to future training and development, make your comments in Part 3 of these Notes.

The value of the discussion will depend to a considerable extent on what you contribute to it. Your manager will be prepared to discuss with you your ideas about your job, and will try to comment on them in a frank and helpful manner.

When the interview is over you may keep this form, or give it to your manager for filing with your personal records.

Part 1 Before the interview:

1. Taking into consideration your performance in your present job, what particular difficulties have you faced? What action can be taken by you or your Manager, to improve your performance?

---

2. Do you believe that you have abilities that can be better utilised than at present? In what ways might your job need to be changed to make this possible?

---

3. Which parts of your job give you the most satisfaction?

---

4. What weaknesses, if any, do you feel are apparent from your performance in the job? What can be done to overcome these?

---

5. What do you think that you, pesonally, can do to improve the work of the Branch, Division or Department?

Part 2 Proposed key tasks for coming year – for discussion

1.

2.

3.

4.

5.

Part 3 After the interview

Are there any comments you wish to make arising from the discussion with your Manager?

Example L

This is an example of a review form for secretarial, clerical and administrative employees and is part of a review scheme which has been in operation in a medium-sized organization in the financial sector for the past five years. The scheme is not salary linked and performance ratings are not required.

The main emphasis of the review scheme is on performance improvement and development and takes a results-oriented approach. This is more pronounced in the performance review for management and professional employees but, as the example shows, is still applied to non-management employees, supplemented by behavioural criteria. One third of the review is given up to development needs and training recommendations.

All reviewers must attend appraisal skills workshops before conducting performance reviews. Refresher courses are also provided. The individual jobholder is expected to prepare for the discussion and retains a copy of the completed report.

PRIVATE & CONFIDENTIAL

PERFORMANCE REVIEW

Reviewee name and initials		(Mr/Mrs/Miss)
Review period: From	To	
Date of review interview		

I PERSONAL RECORD

Surname		Initials	Date of birth
Date of commencement	Company/Dept.		Location
Title of present appointment			Date appointed
Summary of main responsibilities			

II PERFORMANCE ANALYSIS

Refer to agreed main tasks/objectives for period and summarize in first column.
In the second column, comment on achievements during the period.

MAIN TASKS/OBJECTIVES	COMMENTS ON ACHIEVEMENTS
1.	
2.	
3.	
4.	

Comment on the following areas of performance, where appropriate.

Quality of work

Volume of work

Flexibility

Team work

Personality

General summary of years performance

MAIN TASKS/OBJECTIVES FOR THE NEXT YEAR
1.
2.
3.
4.

III DEVELOPMENT TRAINING
1. Summary of performance in relation to training
(a) The parts of the job done well
(b) The parts of the job where difficulties arise
2. Is employee capable of performing a job of higher or wider responsibility, given the current level of skill, aptitude and training?
Comment:-
If so, what post would be most suitable?
Does employee aspire to this post?
Has an interest been expressed in a different post or type of work?
3. Training recommendations
Indicate what specific instruction, tuition or training would assist the employee to develop:
Department training:-
Company training:-
Internal Group training:-
External training:-
Other:-

COMMENTS BY SECOND REVIEWER

Prepared by (block caps)	Countersigned by (block caps)
Position	Position
How long have you known him/her?	How long have you known him/her?
Signature	Signature
Date	Date

DISCLOSURE

This space is available to the Reviewee to make any comment on the review.

I have had the opportunity to read this assessment form on

Signed (Reviewee) Date

PERSONNEL DEPARTMENT USE

602

Example M

This form is used for the performance review of all non-management employees in a medium-sized retailing organization. It is part of a performance review system which has recently been revised and standardized across levels of employee.

The format uses graphic rating scales and an overall performance grading. The approach is primarily personality-oriented but includes sections on performance improvement and training requirements. It is not directly salary linked.

The employee signs the completed report and may make additional comments.

CONFIDENTIAL

STAFF PERFORMANCE APPRAISAL

NAME OF STAFF	
POSITION	
MANAGERS NAME	
POSITION	
DEPARTMENT	
STORE	
PERIOD COVERED	
DATE APPOINTED TO PRESENT POSITION	

OVERALL PERFORMANCE ASSESSMENT

My overall assessment of this executive's performance in contributing to the profit of the Company over the last year is:-

u	☐	Performance marked by outstanding ability.
o	☐	Performance is more than acceptable.
i	☐	Acceptable performance.
e	☐	Performance less than acceptable in some aspects of work, but without serious shortcomings.
a	☐	Unacceptable performance, considerable improvement is required to permit the retention of this employee in the present position.
n	☐	Newly appointed - too early to assess performance.

Please comment on any specific factors, such as inexperience, health, age, etc., which affected performance.

Appraiser's Signature

Date

PERFORMANCE CHARACTERISTICS

Reviewing this employee's work performance over the last year, please assess him by putting a tick in the box which best indicates, in your opinion, his performance. For example, if the statement on the right or left side describes his performance well, put a tick in the relevant box. PLEASE TRY TO BE OBJECTIVE:

1 PUNCTUALITY

how regular is this employee's attendance and how punctual is his daily and meal break timekeeping?

Consistant and reliable attendance with no time-keeping problem.						Irregular attendance and unpunctual timekeeping.

2 EFFORT

does this employee put his best effort into carrying out his duties?

Hardworking, enthusiastic employee who puts his best into the job						Inconsistant worker, lacking effort, enthusiasm and drive.

3 INITIATIVE

does this employee do things without having to be asked?

Gets on with the job without having to be asked and makes every effort to find out things he does not know.						Waits to be told what to do and does not find out things for himself.

4 PERSONAL STANDARDS

does this employee's personal standards - appearance, manner and conduct - impress you?

Always cheerful, courteous and smartly dressed.						Frequently uncheerful, discourteous and careless about appearance.

5 RELIABILITY

can you give this employee a task and have complete confidence that it will completed to an acceptable standard without having to stand over him?

Very reliable, requiring little supervision.						Unreliable and erratic, requiring constant supervision.

6 RELATIONSHIPS

how does this employee get on with his fellow staff?

Fits into the team well.						Causes friction and disruption.

7 CO–OPERATION

how easily does this employee accept direction from his superiors?

Accepts direction readily and is always helpful and co-operative.						Resents direction and is generally unhelpful.

8 CUSTOMER SERVICE

what sort of service does this employee give his "customers"?

Goes out of his way to give helpful service.						Not interested in customer care.

9 JOB SKILLS

how skilled is this employee in the technical aspects which are fundamental to the job?

Highly skilled and knowledge of all aspects of the job.						Unskilled and in need of constant assistance.

10 RESPONSIBILITY

how willing is this employee to assume extra responsibility beyond the duties outlined in his job description?

Seeks and accepts extra responsibility willingly.						Avoids further responsibility wherever possible.

11 TASK ACHIEVEMENT

how able is this employee to get a job(s) done in a reasonable time to your satisfaction?

Competently completes assignments in the shortest possible time.						Takes a long time to accomplish a little.

12 CONTRIBUTION

how great a personal contribution has this employee made to the profitable success of the department?

Outstanding contribution to the department's success.						Contribution to department's success insignificant.

AREAS FOR IMPROVEMENT

Please note specific, agreed areas of performance improvement

FURTHER TRAINING OR COUNSELLING

Please note any specific training or counselling requirements needed to achieve improved performance.

COMMENTS BY MANAGER

Has this employee made any notable progress or has he regressed in any particular areas?

Manager's Signature Date

COMMENTS BY EMPLOYEE

Please indicate any comments that you wish to make on this appraisal and sign below to show that you have had an appraisal interview.

Signature Date

COMMENTS BY CONTROLLER

Controller's Signature Date

Example N

This is another example of a scheme used for secretarial, clerical and administrative employees, in a small organization in the paper, printing and publishing industry. The review scheme has been operating for about seven years.

The emphasis is on personal development and the review form incorporates a training and support plan. The format is a mixture of narrative and ratings, only an overall rating of performance being required. Factors influencing performance can also be noted, using a simple check-list. A broad indication of potential is required, again using a check-list. The employee is expected to sign the completed performance review form.

Form PDR
CONFIDENTIAL

PERSONAL DEVELOPMENT REVIEW

NAME	
JOB TITLE	
DEPARTMENT	
PERIOD UNDER REVIEW	1983/84 Financial Year
PERIOD COVERED BY FORWARD PLAN	1984/85 Financial Year
DATE OF REVIEW	
COMPLETED BY	

EXPLANATORY NOTES

BACKGROUND

The PDR is intended to summarise the annual development meeting between each member of staff and their Manager or Supervisor during which they review jointly the individual's training and development activity and work-achievements during the past year and agree Action Plans for training, development and support for the individual during the year ahead.

PLANNING AND PREPARATION

Give your staff advance warning of the meeting. Tell them why you are meeting and what to expect. Consider giving them a blank PDR and asking them to complete the form themselves as a basis for your discussion. Prepare yourself for the meeting by clearing your desk, barring your telephone and spending some time looking at the individual within the context of the year under review.

THE MEETING

Minimise interruptions. Discuss each heading in the PDR in turn. Ask your staff for their own views of their work-achievement and training, development and support needs. Be objective, avoid being judgemental.

COMPLETION

Not every member of your staff will need training and development. Please note NIL returns on the Plan. Some needs identified may be approached through on-job training. Training recommendations need not always be for course attendance. Please complete the Action side of the Training & Support plan; where specific training requirements are identified, the Training Manager should be consulted as to the best way of fulfilling these. The Comments/Assessment side will be completed during the forthcoming year by the Training Manager.

RETURN

Please pass the form when completed to the Personnel Department.

REVIEW OF CURRENT PERFORMANCE

(1) Indicate level of performance achieved during the year under review by ticking the appropriate box.
See last page for definition of categories.

☐ Capacity very under utilised in present job ☐ Outstanding Performance ☐ Fully Competent Performance ☐ Performance Capable of Improvement ☐ Provisional

Note any circumstances that are likely to have affected performance by ticking appropriate box or boxes.

☐ changes in the reviewee's job ☐ changes in the reviewee's department

☐ changes of personnel affecting the reviewee's job ☐ changes within the Company

☐ domestic or health matters ☐ new employee

Briefly comment, if necessary, especially if your assessment of performance is in the top or the provisional categories.

(2) Indicate potential by ticking appropriate box or boxes.

☐ has supervisory or management potential ☐ has talents or strengths unused in present job

☐ has ability to undertake more difficult job ☐ wishes to progress to more difficult and rewarding job

☐ has no present wish to progress further in the Company ☐ need to develop in present job

Comment on above as necessary.

(3) Summarise any training and development needs arising from the performance during the year under review; also bear in mind any training which may be necessary owing to our increased commitment to computerisation, e.g. keyboard training, word processing training, general computer knowledge training.

(4) If the reviewee has any comments to make, they should be made below. Otherwise, he or she should sign below to confirm that the PDR has been agreed.

....

TRAINING AND SUPPORT PLAN **Name** ....

ACTION	COMMENTS/ASSESSMENT

DEFINITION OF CATEGORIES OF LEVELS OF PERFORMANCE

Capacity very under utilised in present job:	Exceptional and consistent high-level performance that could clearly be agreed by anyone who observes this person's work.
Outstanding:	Performance is noticeably better than that required to do the job satisfactorily.
Fully Competent:	Performance consistently results in the job being done satisfactorily.
Improvement Required:	Performance is below that required to do the job satisfactorily.
Provisional:	Almost always a person too new to be performing properly; may also be very poor performance which must improve rapidly if individual is to stay in position.

Example O

This is an example of a form used for the review of graduate trainees. The performance review is carried out twice a year and uses multi-raters.

The format is based on rating scales and uses a mixture of job behaviour and personality ratings. An overall performance rating is required. The assessment is carried out before the review discussion and is used mainly as a counselling device for the trainees. A section is provided for the record of the performance discussion and any development plans. The graduate sees the completed report and signs it.

The scheme has been in use for about four years and has recently been adapted for other non-management, non-manual employees.

10807 SLA

Name . . . .

Job Title . . . .

Dept. No. . . . .

PERSONAL AND CONFIDENTIAL

GRADUATE STAFF APPRAISAL FORM

To . . . . (name) . . . . (Dept. No.)

Immediate Supervisor ☐ A

. . . . (name) . . . . (Dept. No.)

Other Rater ☐ B

Occasion for Appraisal . . . .

Please complete this Form as indicated and in accordance with any amplifying advice from your Personnel Department as soon as possible.

Completed Forms should be returned to:-

. . . .

by . . . .

NOTE: Space is provided on the back of this Form for you to record details of any discussion and decisions arising from this appraisal with the employee concerned. The Form will be returned to you by your Personnel Department in due course with guidance on the nature of feedback to be conducted.

1. ASPECTS OF PERFORMANCE

Please tick the appropriate rating box (A to E) using the following response scale:

The description:-

Applies in all respects . . . . . Tick A
Applies to a large extent. . . . Tick B
Applies to some extent. . . . . Tick C
Barely applies . . . . Tick D
Does NOT apply at all . . . . . Tick E

1.1 PLANNING
☐ N.O. Clearly sees the purpose and objectives of a job and develops a properly structured plan for their achievement.

A	B	C	D	E
☐	☐	☐	☐	☐

1.2 TECHNICAL COMPETENCE
☐ N.O. Has demonstrated an ability to apply technical knowledge and skills to the work situation.

A	B	C	D	E
☐	☐	☐	☐	☐

1.3 ANALYTICAL ABILITY
☐ N.O. Effective in assessing own information requirements to define work problems and resolve them.

A	B	C	D	E
☐	☐	☐	☐	☐

1.4 ORIGINALITY
☐ N.O. Creative and open-minded with novel approaches to problem solving. Willing to challenge the conventional wisdom whenever appropriate.

A	B	C	D	E
☐	☐	☐	☐	☐

1.5 CONTROL
☐ N.O. Clearly identifies factors critical to the success of an assignment. Monitors and reports on these in a timely fashion.

A	B	C	D	E
☐	☐	☐	☐	☐

1.6 APPLICATION
☐ N.O. Displays high degree of personal application to assigned tasks and can be relied upon to complete them against standards required.

A	B	C	D	E
☐	☐	☐	☐	☐

2. OVERALL PERFORMANCE IN PRESENT POST DURING THE PERIOD UNDER REVIEW

Take account of the various aspects of Performance you have just rated and also the extent to which the employee met agreed objectives during the period under review. Tick the one statement which most accurately reflects Performance overall. Add any comments and points for feedback in the space provided.

* EXPLANATIONS TO SUPPORT AN "OUTSTANDING" RATING ARE REQUIRED ON A SEPARATE SHEET, PLEASE ATTACH IT TO THIS FORM.

Comments

NAME .... Dept. No. ....

Box N.O. = No opportunity to demonstrate this behaviour.

Indicate any aspect of performance which is particularly important in your view by underlining the Heading.

		A	B	C	D	E
1.7 ☐ N.O.	WRITTEN WORK Written work clearly identifies purpose of message, is well structured, concise and grammatically correct.	☐	☐	☐	☐	☐
1.8 ☐ N.O.	ORAL COMMUNICATION Expresses himself/herself clearly, concisely and to the point. Able to capture and maintain the interest of the listener.	☐	☐	☐	☐	☐
1.9 ☐ N.O.	RELATIONS WITH MANAGEMENT Communicates openly and readily with his/her own Manager, and not afraid to present his/her views, but in an acceptable manner.	☐	☐	☐	☐	☐
1.10 ☐ N.O.	RELATIONS WITH COLLEAGUES Is acceptable and gets on well with colleagues. Shows evidence of working, influencing and communicating well in a team.	☐	☐	☐	☐	☐
1.11 ☐ N.O.	ABILITY TO LEARN Shows evidence of having acquired knowledge and skills from formal and/or informal training received.	☐	☐	☐	☐	☐
1.12 ☐ N.O.	ADJUSTMENT TO COMPANY Has demonstrated the ability to adapt to the demands, requirements and disciplines of Company life.	☐	☐	☐	☐	☐

		Overall Rating
* OUTSTANDING. Work of a very high quality all round. Contributions far exceed normal requirements.	A	☐
VERY GOOD. Work is generally satisfactory and some aspects of it are extremely good.	B	☐
GOOD. Work is quite acceptable, but very rarely exceeds normal requirements.	C	☐
ACCEPTABLE. Work is acceptable, but some is mediocre or disappointing. There are one or two significant weaknesses.	D	☐
MARGINALLY UNACCEPTABLE. Most work is not of an acceptable standard and there are a number of significant weaknesses.	E	☐
UNACCEPTABLE. Work is of a generally unacceptable standard and there are a large number of major weaknesses.	F	☐

Raters Signature .... Date ....

NOTES: on discussion and decisions arising from the Appraisal. (If you have already completed appropriate Development Paperwork with the Employee this section may be left blank.)

Employee's Signature . . . .

Supervisor's Signature . . . .

APPENDIX 2

METHODOLOGY AND SURVEY POPULATION

Survey sample

The sample population was a stratified random sample of UK organizations in both public and private sectors. The sample was stratified by industry, using the standard industrial classification and drawn from the Kompas Register, Dun and Bradstreet's Guide to Key Enterprises and the Public Authorities Directory. The sampling method yielded a sample population of 800 UK organizations across a wide cross-section of industries and services.

Survey method

Since this survey was intended to update the previous IPM surveys on performance appraisal, it was considered necessary to duplicate the methods used in 1977, ie postal self-completion questionnaires, supplemented by selected follow-up interviews. Minor amendments were made to the 1977 questionnaire, following some exploratory interviewing. As before, a non-personalized covering letter accompanied the questionnaire. This approach enabled direct comparisons between the 1977 and 1985 data collections.

Response rate

Of the 800 questionnaires posted, 307 were completed and returned. In addition 25 letters were received giving reasons for non-participation, making the overall response rate 42 per cent. One returned questionnaire was unusable, giving a final survey population of 306. The 1977 survey yielded 288 usable questionnaires (50 per cent response) so for comparative purposes the 1985 response was satisfactory. In addition 151 organizations submitted examples of their performance review documentation, including 247 review forms and 136 guidelines.

In depth interviewing in 20 of the participating organizations yielded yet further detailed information.

Description of survey population

Size of participating organizations:

Table A1 - Distribution of organizations by size

Number of employees		N	%
500 or less		42	14
501 - 1,000		39	13
1,001 - 5,000		121	40
5,001 - 10,000		37	12
10,001 - 20,000		19	6
Over 20,000		47	15
	Base	306	

Non-response 1 Col %

As shown in Table A1, 40 per cent of respondents came from medium-sized organizations and a further 27 per cent from small organizations (1000 or less employees). The least represented were organizations with 10,000-20,000 employees. Respondents were also asked to indicate whether their contribution represented a total organization, a division or a location.

Table A2 - Distribution of respondents by organization, division or location

		N	%
Total organization		236	77
Division		45	15
Location		21	7
	Base	306	

Non-response 4 Col %

The majority of completed questionnaires represented total organizations. Fifteen per cent represented divisions, the majority of which employed no more than 5,000 employees. There was only a very small minority of locations represented, 50 per cent employing no more than 500 employees.

Standard industrial classification:

Table A3 - Distribution of participating organizations by industry

	N	%
Mining and quarrying	5	2
Bricks, pottery, glass and cement	5	2
Chemical and allied industries	34	11
Metal processing and goods	5	2
Vehicles	4	1
Mechanical and marine engineering	23	8
Electrical and electronic engineering	22	7
Construction	10	3
Timber and furniture	3	1
Paper, printing and publishing	14	5
Textiles, leather, footwear and clothing	9	3
Other manufacturing industries	15	5
Food, drink and tobacco	46	15
Distributive industries	23	8
Gas, electricity and water	6	2
Transport and communication	8	3
Insurance, banking and finance	30	10
Professional and scientific services	2	1
Miscellaneous services	10	3
Public administration and health	32	10
Base	306	
% errors due to rounding		Col %

Table A4 - Distribution of interview sample by industry

	N
Chemical and allied industries	5
Mechanical and marine engineering	2
Electrical and electronic engineering	2
Paper, printing and publishing	2
Textiles, leather, footwear and clothing	1
Distributive industries	1
Insurance, banking and finance	4
Transport and communication	2
Miscellaneous services	1
Public administration	1
Total	20

APPENDIX 3

REFERENCES

1 FLETCHER Clive A and WILLIAMS Richard. Performance appraisal and career development. London, Hutchinson, 1985. (The personnel management series)

2 BANKS Cristina G and MURPHY Kevin R. "Toward narrowing the research-practice gap in performance appraisal." Personnel Psychology. Vol 38, No 2, Summer 1985. pp 335-345

3 MEIDAN Arthur. The appraisal of managerial performance. New York, AMACOM, 1981 (American Management Association management briefing)

4 McGREGOR Douglas. "An uneasy look at performance appraisal." Harvard Business Review. Vol 35, No 3, May-June 1957. pp 89-94

5 DRUCKER Peter F. The practice of management. London, Heinemann, 1955

6 LEVINSON Harry. "Management by objectives: a critique." Training and Development Journal. Vol 26, No 4, April 1972. pp 3-6, 8

7 KOONTZ Harold. "Shortcomings and pitfalls in managing objectives." Management by Objectives. Vol 1, No 3, January 1972. p8

8 YAGER Ed. "A critique of performance appraisal systems." Personnel Journal. Vol 60, No 2, February 1981. pp 129-133

9 GRAVES J Peter. "Let's put appraisal back in performance appraisal: Part 1." Personnel Journal. Vol 61, No 11, November 1982. pp 844-849

10 McGREGOR Douglas. 1957. op cit

11 THORNTON III G C. "Psychometric properties of self-appraisals of job performance." Personnel Psychology. Vol 33, No 2, Summer 1980. pp 263-271

12 MEYER Herbert H. "Self-appraisal of job performance." Personnel Psychology. Vol 33, No 2, Summer 1980. pp 291-295

13 FLETCHER Clive A and WILLIAMS Richard. 1985. op cit

14 PATTEN Thomas H. Pay: employee compensation and incentive plans. New York, Free Press: London, Collier-MacMillan, 1977

15 DAWIS R V. "Personnel assessment from the perspective of the theory of work adjustment." Public Personnel Management. Vol 9, No 4, 1980. pp 268-273

16 RANDELL Gerry, PACKARD Peter and SLATER John. Staff appraisal: a first step to effective leadership. 3rd ed. London, Institute of Personnel Management, 1984

17 DeVRIES David L, MORRISON Ann M, SCHULLMAN Sandra L and GERLACH Michael L. Performance appraisal on the line. Greensboro, NC, Centre for Creative Leadership, 1980

18 BANNER David K and GRABER James M. "Critical issues in performance appraisal." Journal of Management Development. Vol 4, No 1, 1985. pp 26-35

19 GILL Deirdre. Appraising performance: present trends and the next decade. London, Institute of Personnel Management, 1977 (Information report 25)

20 LACHO Kenneth J, STEARNS G Kent and VILLERE Maurice F. "A study of employee appraisal systems of major cities in the United

States." Public Personnel Management. Vol 8, No 2, March-April 1979. pp 111-125

21 CATALANELLO Ralph F and HOOPER John A. "Managerial appraisal." Personnel Administrator. September 1981. pp 75-79

22 EICHEL Evelyn and BENDER Henry E. Performance appraisal: a study of current techniques. New York, American Management Associations, Research and Information Service, 1984

23 BUREAU OF NATIONAL AFFAIRS. Performance appraisal programs. Washington DC, The Bureau, 1983 (Personnel policies forum survey 135)

24 WALKER James. Outside organizations' appraisal arrangements: a survey of 23 organizations. London, Management and Personnel Office, 1983

25 BUREAU OF NATIONAL AFFAIRS. 1983. op cit

26 GILL Deirdre. 1977. op cit

27 RANDELL Gerry et al. 1984. op cit

28 EICHEL Evelyn and BENDER Henry E. 1985. op cit

29 BUREAU OF NATIONAL AFFAIRS. 1983. op cit

30 LACHO Kenneth J et al. 1979. op cit

31 CATALANELLO Ralph F and HOOPER John A. 1981. op cit

32 INCOMES DATA SERVICES LIMITED and INSTITUTE OF PERSONNEL MANAGEMENT. The merit factor: rewarding individual performance. London, IDS, 1985

33 FOSSUM John A _and_ FITCH Mary K. "The effects of individual and contextual attributes on the sizes of recommended salary increases." _Personnel Psychology_. Vol 38, No 3, Autumn 1985. pp 587-602

34 ANSTEY Edgar, FLETCHER Clive A _and_ WALKER James. _Staff appraisal and development_. London, Allen and Unwin, 1976

35 DeVRIES David L et al. 1980. op cit

36 FLETCHER Clive A _and_ WILLIAMS Richard. 1985. op cit

37 BANNER David K _and_ GRABER James M. 1985. op cit

38 MAIER Norman R F. _The appraisal interview: objectives, methods and skills_. New York, London, Wiley. 1958

39 RANDELL Gerry et al. 1984. op cit

40 DeVRIES David L et al. 1980. op cit

41 LANDY Frank J _and_ FARR James L. _The measurement of work performance: methods, theory and applications_. New York, London etc, Academic Press, 1983

42 EICHEL Evelyn _and_ BENDER Henry E. 1985. op cit

43 GILL Deirdre. 1977. op cit

44 WALKER James. 1983. op cit

45 FLANAGAN J C. "The critical incident technique." _Psychological Bulletin_. Vol 51, No 4, July 1954. pp 327-358

46 LANDY Frank J _and_ FARR James L. 1983. op cit

47 Ibid

48 GRUENFIELD Elaine F. Performance appraisal: promise and peril. Ithaca, NY, New York State School of Industrial and Labor Relations. 1981 (Key issues No 25)

49 GILL Deirdre. 1977. op cit

50 TEEL Kenneth S. "Performance appraisal: current trends, persistent progress." Personnel Journal. Vol 59, No 4, April 1980. pp 296-301, 316

51 WALKER James. 1983. op cit

52 DeVRIES David L et al. 1980. op cit

53 McGUIRE Peter J. "Why performance appraisals fail." Personnel Journal. Vol 59, No 9, September 1980. pp 744-746, 762

54 MARGERISON Charles. "A constructive approach to appraisal." Personnel Management. Vol 8, No 7, July 1976. pp 30-34

55 MAIER Norman R F. 1958. op cit

56 ROWE Kay H. "An appraisal of appraisals." Journal of Management Studies. Vol 1, No 1, March 1964. pp 1-25

57 ALLINSON C W. "Training in performance appraisal interviewing: an evaluation study." Journal of Management Studies. Vol 14, No 2, May 1977. pp 179-191

58 Ibid

59 IVANCEVICH John M. "Subordinates' reactions to performance appraisal interviews: a test of feedback and goal-setting techniques." Journal of Applied Psychology. Vol 67, No 5, 1982. pp 581-587

60 STEWART Andrew M _and_ STEWART Valerie. "Beginning appraisal training." _Industrial Training International_. Vol 7, No 7, July 1972. pp 209-211

61 PRYOR Roger. "A fresh approach to performance appraisal." _Personnel Management_. June 1985. pp 37-39

62 RANDELL Gerry et al. 1984. op cit

63 Ibid

64 FLETCHER Clive A. "Interview style and the effectiveness of appraisal." _Occupational Psychology_. Vol 47, No 3 and 4, 1973. pp 225-230

65 WILSTED W D _and_ TAYLOR R L. "Identifying criteria for performance appraisal decisions." _Journal of Management Studies_. Vol 15, No 3, October 1978. pp 255-264

66 KAYE Beverly L _and_ KRANTZ Shelley. "Preparing employees: the missing link in performance appraisal training." _Personnel_. May-June 1982. pp 23-29

67 McHENRY Robert, HOWARD John _and_ McHATTON Mike. _Employee-driven performance appraisal_. Oxford, Robert McHenry Associates. 1984

68 BERNADIN H John _and_ BEATTY R W. _Performance appraisal: assessing human behaviour at work_. Boston, Kent, 1984
Cited in
FERRIS Gerald R et al. "The influence of subordinate age on performance ratings and causal attributions." _Personnel Psychology_. Vol 38, No 3, Autumn 1985. pp 545-557

69 FLETCHER Clive A _and_ WILLIAMS Richard. 1985. op cit

70 THORNTON III G C. 1980. op cit

71 LAZER R I and WIKSTROM W S. Appraising managerial performance: current practices and future directions. New York, The Conference Board, 1977

72 FELDMAN Jack M. "Beyond attribution theory: cognitive processes in performance appraisal." Journal of Applied Psychology. Vol 66, No 2, 1981. pp 127-148

73 STEWART Valerie and STEWART Andrew M. Managing the poor performer. Aldershot, Hants, Gower, 1982

74 Ibid

75 FLETCHER Clive A. 1973. op cit

76 RANDELL Gerry et al. 1984. op cit

77 LANDY Frank J and FARR James L. 1984. op cit

78 FOURNIES F AND ASSOCIATES INC. Performance appraisal-design manual. Bridgewater, NJ, F Fournies, 1983

79 GILL Deirdre. 1977. op cit

80 FLETCHER Clive A and WILLIAMS Richard. 1984. op cit

81 GILL Deirdre. 1977. op cit

82 GILL Deirdre, UNGERSON Bernard and THAKUR Manab. Performance appraisal in perspective: a survey of current practice. London, Institute of Personnel Management, 1973 (Information Report 14)

83 STEWART Andrew M and STEWART Valerie. Tomorrow's managers today: the identification and development of management potential. 2nd ed. London, Institute of Personnel Management, 1981

84 LAZER R I and WIKSTROM W S. 1977. op cit

85 Ibid

86 YAGER Ed. 1981. op cit

87 LAWLER III Edward E, MOHRMAN Jr Allan M and RESNICK Susan M. "Performance appraisal revisited." Organizational Dynamics. Summer 1984. pp 20-35

88 BERNADIN H John and KLATT Lawrence A. "Managerial appraisal systems: has practice caught up to the state of the art? Personnel Administrator. November 1985. pp 79-86

89 LANZA Peggy. "Team appraisals." Personnel Journal. Vol 64, No 3, March 1985. pp 47-51

90 GILBERT G R. "Performance appraisal and organizational practice: a post reform review." Public Personnel Management. Vol 11, No 4, Winter 1982. pp 318-321

91 DeVRIES David L et al. 1980. op cit